POSITIVE P

a survival guide

PAT REES

Attic Press
Dublin

First published in Ireland in 1991 by
Attic Press
44 East Essex Street
Dublin 2

British Library Cataloguing in Publication Data
Rees, Pat
   Positive parenting.
   1.   Parenthood
   I.   Title
   649.1

   ISBN 1-85594-018-3

Cover Design: Michelle Cullen, Attic Press
Cover and in-text illustrations: Sue Gerber
Origination: Attic Press
Printing: The Guernsey Press Co Ltd

To my parents Peg and Jack
for all their love.

A big thank you to Sue Gerber who, with her inspired artwork and warmth, allowed the vision I had of the book to come true. My heartfelt thanks go out to Anne Roper and Dr Maura Woods for reading and advising me on the book. To Mary Hyland for taking care of my children in the most loving way. To Pauline Daly for friendship and support. To Denis Cahallane and Bob McMullan for guiding me through the perils of my new computer. Lastly (but first and foremost really) to my darling husband Denis, my thanks for writing the piece on fatherhood and without whose love, support and friendship this book would never have been written. And oodles of love, hugs and kisses to my children Sarah, Rory and Genevieve who are the treasures of my life.

Contents

The positive parenting approach

I have written this book, not as a complete childcare book, as there are plenty of these available to tell us how to care for our little ones. Instead, I have gathered hints and tips and words of wisdom that have been learned, tried and tested by myself and other parents. I have put together tips usually left out of basic care books, practical things I have learned from my work as a nurse, mother and parent adviser.

Positive Parenting is a practical self-help guide and covers the various stages of child rearing, offering help and advice on common difficulties you may encounter as a parent. You can find the advice you need without having to wade through whole chapters - simply refer to the topic you want, and positive, practical tips are listed step by step, point by point.

The relationship between a parent and child is unique. No one can ever tell you what to do fully, so along with these practical hints, I would always tell you to look inside your heart for the right answer, and always to be aware of your own needs and your own special insight into your child.

Being a parent

Being a parent is the most difficult, yet the most fulfilling thing I have done in my life. I have read enough books to fill a large room on what to do, and how to do it. No book can encompass the many problems encountered on the journey through parenthood. Funnily enough, the more we have to look for advice, the less we like it because part of us thinks parenting is all natural and we should be able to cope with it on our own. Knowing a few handy hints makes parenthood more enjoyable and less traumatic. If you try to see life through the eyes of your child, it will give you a good insight on parenthood and life itself - *enjoy it!*

Pre-conceptual care

Pre-conceptual care is basically care of the parents prior to even getting pregnant. So let's start at the very beginning. Why is pre-conceptual care important? Ask yourself:

Do you want to give your baby the best possible start in life?

Do you want to be fit during pregnancy and avoid complications during pregnancy and birth?

If the answer is 'Yes' it's only sensible for both parents to be as fit and healthy as possible. So you start with a healthy egg and sperm. It is during the first twelve weeks that all the baby's vital body parts are developing. Your baby has started to develop before you even get a positive pregnancy test. That's why pre-conceptual care is so important.

Tips to ensure you are fit enough to get pregnant

* Eat a good, **well-balanced diet**, containing milk, dairy products, wholemeal breads, brown rice, wholewheat pasta and protein foods such as meat, seafood and eggs. Other protein alternatives are peas, beans, lentils, nuts and seeds. Fresh vegetables and fruits are a must and whenever appropriate eat the whole fruit including skins.

* **Avoid highly refined food** and carbohydrates, such as white bread, white flour, white sugar and soft, fizzy drinks.

* Try to eat 50% of your fruit and vegetables **raw**. Cooking often destroys vitamin and mineral content.

* Don't store **vegetables and fruit** for too long, again it destroys the nutrients in food.

* **Eat regularly** and **drink plenty of liquids**, especially water, but go easy on tea and coffee.

* **Vitamin and mineral supplements** taken for three months prior to getting pregnant are thought to reduce the chance of having a baby with problems and also ensure that you won't be lacking essential nutrients when you conceive.

* If over-weight, **do not go on a strict diet**, it is dangerous for your baby. Just eat sensibly and you should healthily lose those extra pounds.

* **Stop smoking!** Otherwise you are putting your baby at risk. Potential fathers should also stop smoking as it can

reduce the quality of sperm. If you can't stop smoking altogether, cut it down to five daily. Every little helps.

* **Alcohol** can be dangerous to your unborn baby. Experts differ as to what levels of alcohol are dangerous. Not drinking any alcohol is best, but the odd glass of wine or beer should be OK - spirits are too strong.

* Get a **medical check-up,** including a smear test, before you conceive to ensure you are healthy. Any vaginal or urinary infections or problems should be looked after before conceiving.

* **Come off the contraceptive pill** for at least six months before even trying to get pregnant.

* Check you are immune to **Rubella.**

* Some doctors recommend being immunised against **influenza** if you are likely to get pregnant in the winter.

* If you or your family has an **allergy** problem, it is a good idea to track down the cause before you get pregnant.

* Any **drug** or **medication** may harm the developing baby so come off all medication, unless you have received advice from your GP stating it is OK to stay on it.

* Get plenty of **fresh air and exercise.**

* Get enough **sleep** and rest.

* Parents should prepare for pregnancy together to set a good standard for your future family fitness.

* Space out your pregnancies. It is advisable to wait one or two years (at least) between the birth of one baby and a subsequent pregnancy.

* Do your best to be in a **calm** state. If you are over-anxious, depressed or stressed, seek help before getting pregnant.

* If you have had any previous pregnancy problems or a baby with a congenital problem, you may like to contact FORESIGHT - the pre-conceptual care association (address at the back of this book) who do a booklet on *Guidelines for future parents.*

Antenatal care

When we discover we are pregnant our feelings can fluctuate between shock, horror, and being absolutely thrilled, depending on whether we expected the news or not. There is so much to learn and yet the most important thing is to enjoy it. Decisions about the type of birth and where you want to have the baby, whether you want to breast or bottle feed, are very personal ones. They have a lot to do with your own preferences, likes, dislikes and lifestyle. Whatever you decide about antenatal care, the pregnancy, birth and subsequent care of your baby, you should find out and talk about all the options open to you during this antenatal period. The aim is to get enough knowledge so you are confident and feel in control and can therefore enjoy your own unique pregnancy and birth.

Here is a brief guide to your antenatal care, including some minor disorders you may encounter.

Tips
* Educate yourself on all that is happening to your body.

* Go to good **antenatal classes**, in the hospital and privately too if you can (see CHILDBIRTH TRUST addresses at the back of this book). You cannot be over-prepared for pregnancy.

* Bring your partner or friend along to antenatal classes so that they know what to expect and how to help you.

* Classes should contain **education, relaxation** and **exercise** as well as providing **support**.

* When going to your **doctor**, midwife or class, take along a list of the questions you would like to ask.

* You should be seen monthly by your doctor up to the seventh month, then fortnightly to the eighth month, then weekly until birth.

Look after yourself
* Do some form of **exercise** two or three times a week. Carry on with your normal sport, once it is not too strenuous, until it starts to feel uncomfortable. You could go swimming, a great sport for pregnant women, or simply go for an hour's walk. You can also try exercises specifically designed for the pregnant woman. There are plenty of books and videos available to show you how to do them - look around for what suits you.

* **Diet** is especially important when you are pregnant. You do need a wholesome well-balanced diet. Eat more wholegrain products, wholemeal bread, fresh fruit and vegetables, lean meat, fish and chicken, grains and beans, milk, cheese and yoghurt. Eat less fatty foods, less salt in cooking (or in snacks like crisps) and generally less refined sugar products such as cakes or biscuits.

* Don't 'eat for two' and avoid large meals and spicy or fried foods.

* Eating small meals on a regular basis is best.

* **Fluids** are important too - take a daily pint of milk if you can, or else take milk products. Drink at least six glasses of fluid daily. I favour ordinary water, or mineral water, it is so cleansing, and you could add some fruit juice, or try herbal teas (raspberry leaf is great for pregnancy), but not too much tea or coffee.

* Doctors differ as to whether taking **vitamin and mineral supplements** does any good. But there are ones specially prepared for pregnant women. I took them for two of my pregnancies and felt great and my babies thrived - it is up to you. Certainly pregnant women need plenty of extra iron, folic acid, and calcium in their diet and if you think you are not getting enough, supplements may be the answer.

* Most doctors think it is advisable to take extra **iron** for second or subsequent pregnancies. Some iron supplements can cause side effects such as bowel problems, so look around for the gentlest for your system (if you have problems contact NATURESWAY, address at the back of this book).

* **Weight gain** from 20lb to 28lb, depending on your size, is acceptable - try to stick to it.

* **Stop smoking,** and if you can't stop then cut down. Research shows it may harm your baby. Avoid a very smoky atmosphere as even passive smoking affects your baby.

* **Alcohol** - the best advice, although believe me I know it is hard to take, is not to drink any alcohol from the time you try to conceive until after your baby is born. But the odd glass of wine or beer is not likely to do much harm. The first three months of pregnancy is the most important time to avoid alcohol.

* It pays to be careful of certain diseases during pregnancy. **Rubella** - check that you are immune prior to pregnancy

11

and avoid all contact with it whilst pregnant.
Toxoplasmosis - can be caught from infected animals,
especially cats, avoid contact with their motions.
Listeriosis - an infection caused by bacteria which may
be present in badly stored food. It may be worth avoiding
prepared foods such as pâté, cooked meats and ripe soft
cheeses, just to be on the safe side.

* **X-Rays** are best avoided.

* No **medication** should be taken unless specifically
  prescribed by your doctor. This includes aspirin,
  headache tablets, and over-the-counter remedies for the
  common cold.

* Check up what **benefits** you are entitled to - they differ
  from country to country (DEPARTMENT OF SOCIAL
  WELFARE addresses at the back of this book).

* **Partners** may feel left out during pregnancy. They
  should make a special effort to be involved. Go to the
  classes together, read books about children, share in the
  whole experience.

* Care of the **breasts** is important if you intend to
  breastfeed. Get a good fitting bra (breast size tends to
  enlarge). Massage with cream after bathing. During late
  pregnancy, clear fluid will leak from your nipples, this
  needs to be cleaned away with water. Also, to promote
  milk flow later on, press the area around nipples with
  your thumb and forefingers for a few seconds to express
  any colostrum, or get your partner to suckle your breasts
  - that can be an enjoyable way to prepare you for
  breastfeeding.

* If you intend to have an active, **natural birth**, squatting
  regularly is a good exercise.

* Good **posture** is important. Ensure you sit on
  comfortable chairs and stand correctly. Always bend
  your knees when lifting anything, and keep your spine
  straight. Avoid high-heeled shoes. Taking these measures
  will help avoid backache.

* **Extra sleep** and rest is needed. Put your feet up
  whenever you can and avoid standing for long periods.
  Take afternoon naps. For comfort, use pillows to prop
  you up or support your back or tummy.

* **Sex in pregnancy** is fine, but some postions may feel
  uncomfortable, so experiment. For a few women who
  have had troubled pregnancies sex may be restricted - ask
  your doctor's advice if in doubt.

* **Pelvic floor exercises** should be done by all women, but they are especially important during and after pregnancy. Otherwise the pelvic muscles can get weak and cause problems like stress incontinence or prolapse later on. Do them daily.

* Learn a **relaxation** technique that you can do daily, have a relaxed pregnancy and birth. This makes for a relaxed and happy baby.

* **Be kind to yourself** during pregnancy. When we are pregnant our emotions tend to go up and down and feelings can get strong and out of control sometimes. Try not to take on anything too stressful. Relax, take life easy. Talk to your partner or other mothers if things get on top of you.

Minor disorders in pregnancy

* **Nausea** or **vomiting** starting from the fifth week and easing into the thirteenth week is normal, although it may not feel it. Eat a plain biscuit and have a refreshing drink before you get out of bed in the morning (partners please note). Eat small amounts frequently. Carry around a packet of crackers to chew when your stomach is empty. Ginger grated in boiled water made into a brew is a natural remedy - add honey to taste, or suck crystallised ginger. Vitamin B6 is supposed to help, foods high in it are wheatgerm and whole foods, and marmite on brown bread makes a tasty snack too. If nausea continues homoeopathists have very good remedies to help (contact the COMPLEMENTARY MEDICAL ASSOCIATION, addresses at the back of this book).

* **Varicose veins** of the legs or back passage (piles) or vulva can occur. Put your feet up when resting, and wear support tights - put them on before getting out of bed. Do foot exercises. Avoid constipation. Your doctor may advise you to wear support for vulvar veins and avoid excess weight gain.

* **Heartburn.** Again, eat a little, often, and avoid spicy and fried foods as these generally make it worse. Antacids can be prescribed by your doctor, and homoeopathic remedies can also help.

* **Frequency of urine** commonly occurs during early pregnancy and then again in late pregnancy due to pressure from the womb. If accompanied by pain or a temperature, see your doctor as it could indicate a urinary infection.

13

* Swelling of the feet may occur due to **fluid retention**. Raise your feet when sitting, do foot exercises, avoid standing and raise the foot of your bed (so long as you do not have high blood pressure). Wear support tights.

* **Bleeding gums** can occur due to increased sensitivity and plaque build-up. Massage and brush teeth daily. Use a soft bristle brush and see your dentist for a check up.

* **Itchy skin** is due to the growing stomach and stretching skin. Moisturise daily with oil or cream. To avoid stretch marks, knead and rub in oil daily, and do not put on too much weight.

* **Vaginal discharge** is always increased during pregnancy. Wear natural fibres such as cotton, but if your vagina gets itchy or sore or if the discharge is smelly or has a funny colour, go to your doctor as you may have a vaginal infection.

* There are many more discomforts of pregnancy that you may or may not get. If ever you are worried that something is not normal, ask your doctor or midwife for advice. It always pays to be sure rather than sorry.

Coming home
after the baby is born

Coming home with a baby to care for can be a shock to the system. Everything in hospital was so organised, advice was at hand, so was all the support you needed. Now you are on your own. This precious baby who cries at will is in your total care and it can be frightening. Try to work out some sort of routine for feeding and changing the baby and keeping the house generally ticking over. You may feel a bit emotionally overwrought, this is only natural. Feelings of inadequacy, guilt, or being unable to cope are common. Rid yourself of the illusion that everything in the garden is rosy for every other parent. All of us have a mixture of feelings of absolute love and sweetness as well as despair with our wonderful babies at different times. It is a time for adjustment for everyone and despite its downside, may also be one of the happiest periods of your life, as you watch your 'darling baby' discover the world.

Tips
* **Bonding.** A newborn baby sleeps most of the day, so try to spend all of the baby's waking hours together in close contact.

* **Eye-to-eye contact** is very important. Your baby recognises your outlines within twenty-four hours.

* **Smell.** Babies love your smell.

* Use a sling or shawl to keep the **physical contact**. Babies love this. It is like being back in the womb.

* **Speak, sing, hum** to your baby. They are used to hearing it, they have been listening to you for months already. It is comforting.

* **Rest** and **relaxation** daily is essential for the new mother. Use the relaxation techniques taught in your antenatal classes.

* Rest for at least one hour a day. Use the time to do your **pelvic exercises**.

* **Feeding, changing, bathing** can take up to seven hours a day. You may feel like that's all you are doing - it's normal.

* Have a **changing box** or area containing all your baby's needs and keep it stocked up.

* Most newborn babies love to be wrapped up well and snugly. But be sure your baby doesn't get **overheated** if in a warm room. Unlike adults, babies do not adjust well to changes in temperatures.

* **Top-tail** every day (wash face and bottom), but a daily bath is not necessary. When you do bathe baby, ensure the room is warm, 85F (29.5C) or above.

* Be sure to **dry** all the tricky skin folds thoroughly, watch the areas under the arms and neck that can often get sore.

* Organise **post-natal support**, know who will be there to help for the first few weeks. Every new parent needs a network of support. Have a list of trusted friends to phone and keep their numbers handy.

* **Share your feelings**, especially if you feel despondent.

* **Delegate** as much as you can - shopping, hoovering, etc.

* Make **mothercare** a priority and an essential part of your babycare routine. Leave the rest to others.

* **Buy in bulk** where feasible. Have a stock of convenience foods so you don't have to go shopping too often.

* If possible, buy enough baby products in for one month.

* Convince yourself that having a tidy house is not as important as having a happy mother and contented baby.

* **Go to bed early**, don't try and burn the candle at both ends. Plenty of sleep will help you be more patient with the baby and other children.

* Remember there is life on the other side. The world may seem as if it is revolving around your newborn baby. But keep up your outside interests. This time passes as your baby grows.

* **Never feel guilty** about not doing this or that or not being a good enough parent. Guilt is an unproductive emotion that helps no one. In your baby's eyes you are a super parent.

Establishing a routine

Here's a suggested routine for caring for a baby approximately twelve weeks old. I have added a little brother to show how you can cope with two.

6:00am	Feed and change baby.
7:30am	Wake toddler, give him his morning drink. A little play all together, settle baby down.
7:45am	Get toddler up, washed and dressed and start breakfast. (Baby sleeps or enjoys the spectacle).
8:30am	Clear away, play with toddler. Organise yourself, try and rest or relax.
10:30am	Toddler can have a nap or rest. Feed baby, full breakfast, play and cuddle.
11:30am	Get toddler up, time together, house duties.
12:30pm	Lunch.
2:30pm	Feed baby, change.
3:00pm	Go for a walk or visit friends.
4:30pm	Dinner time for toddler.
5:30pm	Feed, change baby.
7:30pm	Bedtime for toddler.
8:00pm	Feed, change baby as necessary.
8:30pm	Dinner, rest or relax.
11:00pm	Feed, change baby.

Your evening meal can be slotted in any time to suit your evening routine. I always preferred to relax and eat after they were all in bed.

Tips to help

* Let everyone know your routine, so they do not disturb your rest periods.

* Put up a sign saying *do not disturb* or *we are asleep - call again.*

* Take the phone off the hook when resting.

* Parents should have time alone together too, for a walk, dinner together for an intimate chat, even a little romantic chat on the phone.

* Go out together for a date alone every week.

* Find out about all the local Mother-Toddler groups or any organised **help agencies** near you.

* Babies love **sound** - soothing music can help comfort a baby. Turning a hoover on can work wonders. They love the sound of your voice too - talk to them!

* Do not keep the house unnaturally quiet so baby can sleep, otherwise you'll always have to do it.

* You cannot spoil a newborn baby, stay close.

* It is not good to leave babies to cry for long periods. It does not exercise their lungs. They cry because they need something.

* Something **bright** and **colourful** in the cot gives babies something to look at and enjoy.

* **Music** can be a great therapy for both mother and baby. It helps both of you unwind, so put on a cassette you really like - and enjoy it.

* Prepare the **nappy-changing area** carefully. Use a raised area, at a good height, and keep the lotions, flannels and wipes at one side and buckets and bins at the other. Keep lots of clean nappies to hand.

* Always have a **going out bag** packed and ready with all your baby's needs for outings, so if you get the offer of a trip you can go and enjoy yourself, or just visit a friend if things get on top of you.

* Your baby is unique and may want to determine her/his own feeding and **sleeping patterns**. Adjust your routine to fit around baby's natural flow.

* It may help to write out a list of **priorities**, things that must be done in your day, in order of importance and tackle them as you can around your baby's sleep and feed routine.

* Finally, remember there is no single pre-determined routine with a baby, only what suits each new parent and baby. Your routine will change as your baby grows, and will end up reflecting your own personality and priorities. That is natural and normal. Be as easy-going with yourself as you can, don't set yourself standards that will put pressure on you.

Breastfeeding

Breastfeeding gives the nourishment most suited to your baby's digestive system. All animals instinctively seek a mother's nipple when born. Although babies cannot see properly at first, they can smell and hear you, so the warmth of your body, skin contact, and the security of your nipple forms a very important bond between you both. If you decide to breastfeed your baby, success really depends on you. Some hospitals and staff give great support, others do not, the staff may not have the time to assist you to feed on demand. So make sure you are well informed before the birth. Then you will be confident - take any leaflets or information books with you to guide you. The LA LECHE LEAGUE of Ireland and the UK gives great support to women breastfeeding or wishing to breastfeed (addresses at the back of this book).

Hints and facts to help make breastfeeding a success

Preparation * Prepare your nipple from mid-pregnancy; after bathing rub each nipple (do not use soap on the nipple as it can cause dryness) with a terry cloth. Then press and pull the dark skin around the nipple (areola) with your thumb and fingers, mimicking expression and feeding. Do gentle breast massage. Moisturise with cream or oil (sunflower oil will do - but don't use anything containing perfume).

* When making love, as a normal part of love making, let your partner caress and suck your nipples.

* If your nipples are inverted try to draw them out. Discuss getting a nipple shield with your midwife. Sunlight to the breast in short very carefully timed amounts can help toughen up nipples and breast too.

Feeding * Baby should be put to the breast immediately after birth, even before the cord is cut - it helps deliver the placenta (after birth). The baby's sucking reflex is at its most intense in the first twenty-four hours of life, so the sooner you put the baby to the breast the better.

* Lie on your side and curl up slightly so your baby fits nicely into the crook of your arm. Cupping your breast and offering it by brushing your nipple lightly on your baby's lips encourages baby to open her/his mouth.

* Ensure baby is on the breast properly. The nipple and areola should fit inside the mouth, the tongue should be down and baby's head supported so your breast is not dragged, as otherwise you'll get sore.

* Faulty positioning of the baby on the breast causes an awful lot of sore nipples, so be careful, get guidance as necessary. Support the breast and baby's head well.

* The fluid present in your breast at birth is called colostrum. The quantity looks small but it's full of goodness.

* Sometimes, newborn babies don't seem to be interested at first, don't be put off. Letting them lick and nuzzle your nipple and giving them lots of cuddles is fine.

* Let the baby suckle each breast for a while. I don't believe in limiting the time too much, especially on the first day of life. Five to fifteen minutes each side every two or three hours can be expected.

* To persuade the baby to release the nipple, don't just pull away (Ouch!), break the suction by pressing the baby's jaw, or easing the mouth so air gets in and releases the suction.

* Feed on demand. Keep baby beside your bed or ask for her/him to be brought to you as necessary.

* On the third day the milk comes in. The breasts can then become hard and heavy, full of milk. Frequent feeds relieve this, express a bit before you start so baby can get a good grip.

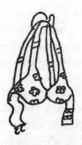

* The flow can be started by massaging in the bath, or massaging before the feeding commences.

* Be patient and persevere. The milk supply will settle down to an amount to satisfy demand.

* If ever extra water or fluids are needed give them after feeds.

* A nursing mother needs adequate rest, a nourishing diet and plenty of fluids. And a good supporting front fastening bra.

* I found that wearing big colourful beads whilst breastfeeding kept the baby occupied.

Problems

Sore nipples * First check **positioning** and **support**. Change position at each feed - changing puts pressure on a different part of the nipple. Expose your nipples to the fresh air and sun, not too much sun. A very ocasional use of sunlamp may help too, but only for very short periods. Calandula ointment is good to heal sore or slightly cracked nipples. Do hand expression if necessary to rest the nipple and breast.

* To ease the pain, wrap crushed ice in a flannel and hold it to the nipple before sucking commences. If **soreness** persists see your GP - it could be caused by thrush.

Other * A **plugged milk duct** presents itself as a painful lump or swelling on your breast. It could be caused by bad positioning when feeding, a prolonged time between feeds, or by wearing a tight bra. To treat it, apply heat, get plenty of rest and give frequent feeds. Sit in a warm bath and relax, gently massage your breast and express milk and encourage the baby to completely empty you at each feed. If the problem persists, contact your GP.

Please note * Breastfeeding naturally, frequently and on demand day and night can provide a lot of protection against another pregnancy. But once the feeding stretches out over the three to four hour period or once solid food is introduced, ovulation may occur even if periods have not commenced. So use another form of **contraception**, for example condoms.

Bottle feeding

Bottle feeding takes a certain amount of good management. The last thing you want is to be making up a bottle feed with a hungry baby screaming down your ear. That's how accidents occur, but with a little bit of forethought and a practical routine, bottle feeding your newborn becomes second nature. One of its good points is that you don't have to be the one to do it all the time - get help.

Equipment you may need starting off

* Six to eight bottles and teats and a sterilising unit or lidded container large enough to hold half of the bottles. I have been known to use large ice cream containers on a temporary basis. You also need sterilising tablets or solution, a bottle brush, a measuring jug (if you don't have one, you can measure milk straight into the bottle), plastic spoon, salt, and a plastic knife. You can buy kits containing all the equipment together.

* Rinse everything in cold water before sterilising.

* Decide on what method of sterilising to use - the **cold method**, using sterilising tablets or solution, I personally found very handy.

* If using **sterilising solution** leave for the stated amount of time, and don't put any equipment in before the tablet is fully dissolved.

* Be sure that all the equipment is fully submerged by the water. Be sure no air bubbles are left. I always used warm water, although some recommend cold water.

* Other methods include **boiling** or **steaming**. For a steam steriliser buy the whole pack at the chemist and read instructions carefully. The unit is expensive, but it saves a lot on sterilising solutions in the future so is worth considering.

* If you choose the **boiling method** every single item used for feeding must be boiled for ten minutes before using it. Then leave in the pan whatever you are not using.

* Whatever method you use everything must be washed in hot soapy water and given a good scrub with the brush. Use **salt** to clean the teat but rinse well afterwards.

* Make up six bottles together - it saves time and effort.

Making up the bottles

* Wash your hands.
* Drain or shake the excess fluid off the bottles, but do not rinse or dry them, or germs will get on them. You can rinse them through with the boiled water if you like.
* Boil a kettle of water and allow to cool a little while.
* Decide how much **formula** your baby needs. For example at two to three months, most babies need 180-210 mls (6-7 oz) at five feeds. This varies from baby to baby, depending on weight and appetite. The amounts are written on the tins of formula.
* Measure the amount of water into each bottle first then add the correct amount of formula, measuring the exact amount of powder, levelling it off with the plastic knife. When you have the two together give the bottle a good shake. Repeat the procedure until all the bottles are prepared.
* Keep all the day's prepared bottles in the fridge until they are needed, allowing them to cool before refrigerating. It may take a while to do it all in the beginning but it gets easier with practice.
* Deciding which formula to use is really a personal choice - have a look around the shops beforehand and ask other parents' opinion. Don't keep changing brands though, unless the one you chose obviously does not suit your baby.
* Remove the bottle from the fridge half an hour before it is needed, or stand it in a bowl of hot water to warm it quickly. But keep it covered. Be very careful if you use a microwave. The milk inside the bottle can be very hot and the bottle could still feel cool; babies' mouths have been severely burned in this way, so extreme caution is necessary and I would advise you *not* to risk doing it.
* Keep the sterilising unit near the sink for convenience.
* You can use discarded sterilising solution for soaking other things such as dish cloths.
* You must change the solution every twenty-four hours.
* Do not put metal in the steriliser. It reacts with the solution.

Feeding your baby

* This is the enjoyable part, a time to savour, a time to cuddle close to your baby and get acquainted. Try to make it a time when you can sit and relax, make yourself and the baby comfortable and enjoy getting to know each other.

* Test the **temperature** by pouring a drop of milk from the bottle on the inside of your wrist, it should not feel too hot or cold.

* Check the **flow** coming out - it should flow out at several drops a second. A continuous stream is too much, and a slow drip means your baby will have to work too hard and will get windy and tired. Adjust the hole if necessary, using a red hot needle.

* **Talk** to your baby during feeding, they love it!

* Sit baby up for **wind** once or twice during the feed (more often for a windy or newborn baby). Then move her/him on your other arm for a new view.

* When offering the bottle, tilt the bottle so there is always milk in the teat and your baby is not swallowing air.

* Have a tissue or cloth handy in case baby brings up a little feed. Have everything you need near you so you don't have to move.

* Never leave a baby alone when feeding - s/he could choke.

* Babies know when they need a rest or have had enough - do not force feed.

* Milk left standing around will go off. Throw it away if it has been standing more than an hour, or keep it in the fridge. Throw away any milk the baby does not finish.

* Do not give a baby under twelve months old ordinary cow's milk.

* In the summer, babies may cry between feeds because they are thirsty. **Cooled boiled water**, or **diluted juice** may be given once the baby is over ten weeks.

* Babies are not toys - they shouldn't be passed around to feed. It is best that a limited number of people feed them until they get older. It protects them from germs and develops **bonds** with those nearest.

* **Never add extra formula** or cereal to the baby's bottle.

* Teats should be renewed on a regular basis.

* Try to get into a regular **routine** of washing, sterilising and making up bottles, morning and evening.

* Do not forget that precious time when you bottle feed your baby and make the most of it. As you and baby get older it will be one of your treasured memories.

Introducing solid food

With a bit of extra iron and perhaps, in some cases, a vitamin supplement, babies could go on just drinking milk and be healthy and happy all their lives. But it wouldn't be very natural, social or practical if they did. I'm stretching a point, of course, but all the same don't be in too much of a hurry to introduce solid food. In most parts of the world, it's not introduced until the end of the first year. Weaning is a time for new tastes and textures, and an adventure of colour and feelings. Do make it a fun adventure, eating is an enjoyable pastime. Be wise in your selection of foodstuffs right from the word go. Start as you mean to go on - it's a great opportunity to learn good eating habits that could last a life-time. A healthy diet from birth, based on unrefined food, avoiding too much sugar, salt and fats will be one of the best gifts you can give your child. Nourishing food need not be expensive - despite the pressures from the advertising world to buy readymade goods, our own natural food can be every bit as convenient.

I know many of us parents find life so full it's handy to have these prepared foods at times. We may not be able to follow the ideal diet all the time but at least we should be aware of that ideal diet and work towards it.

Try to give your children a diet with plenty of fresh produce rich in fibre and nutrients, avoiding refined foods, salts, sugar, white flour, artificial additives and preservatives, saturated fats and oils. Good food is the fuel that's needed for good health - don't forget it.

Weaning or starting solid food

When * Starting solid food varies from four to six months, but babies pick their own time. I think six months old is time enough.

* Look for signs that your baby may be ready to introduce mixed feeding, for example:
    - wanting more frequent milk feeds
    - still being hungry after feeds
    - showing an interest in what people are eating
    - teething and mouthing at objects

* If your baby completely rejects the purée foods from a spoon, delay it a little longer. Don't hurry! Relax.

How * Use chairs that are **comfortable** for both you and baby.

* Be **organised**. Large plastic backed bibs with a shelf are great in case things get messy.

* Are there any **allergies** in either parent's family? If so, it may be wise to find them out beforehand, delay certain foodstuffs if necessary, consult your doctor. Foods that can cause trouble include eggs, wheat and cow's milk.

* Choose a time in the day when you are not rushed.

* Some parents find the **lunch time feed** a good one to start with.

* Start by giving a little milk, breast or bottle. For example, give half of the bottle or one side of the breast, then offer solid food from a spoon. Gradually offer less milk as the amount of solid food is increased.

* **Purée vegetables** (potatoes, cauliflowers, carrots) or fruit make good introductory foods.

* Sieve the food using a manual food blender, a sieve or an electric blender for large amounts and freeze it in small amounts in an ice cube tray. Home-made purée lasts in the fridge for two days. Frozen food can be kept for one month in a deep freeze.

* Only one teaspoon should be offered at first.

* Increase amounts very slowly, decreasing milk at the same time.

* Be sure food is of a smooth consistency, almost semi-liquid at first.

* Baby will most probably be slow to start, will suck the spoon and play at spitting food out at first. That's natural and normal.

* Offer different tastes but don't force babies to eat something they don't like.

* Introduce each new food **individually** so any food that doesn't agree with your baby can be readily identified. Offer new tastes about every third day.

* As you increase variety and amounts, work towards having **fish** included in the diet, followed by **meat** at age eight to ten months so that baby is having a dinner and pudding about two to three months after the initial introduction of food.

* Offer **fruit juice** and **water** by the cup at about five months old. Re-try a few days later if baby rejects it at first.

* Regularly give diluted fruit juice or water with meals instead of the breast or bottle.

* At about nine to twelve months your baby can be having three meals daily with just breast or bottle in the mornings and evenings. This is just a general guide - all babies differ.

* Encourage babies to **feed themselves**. As soon as they can hold a spoon let them. Buy a **suction bowl** or use a suction soap holder to make it easier for them.

* Pets' divided **section bowls** are great - keep separate of course, put baby's name on it.

* Give baby a spoon in each hand if s/he likes. Use round-edged plasic spoons.

* A friendly calm atmosphere at meal times can save a lot of problems later on. Over-anxiety can start conflicts and a bad pattern could commence.

* Do **sterilise** the baby's feeding equipment at first.

* Packets, tins or jars of food are very useful when travelling or when others babysit.

* Gradually reduce the sieving leaving small lumps as time goes on - say at eight months old.

* Toasted crusts, slices of carrot or apple can be introduced around ten months.

* Do talk to your baby, 'look at this lovely orange carrot, do you like it? Here. Smell it, taste it, it's lovely'- and smile! **Be positive!**

* Start teaching baby to drink from a cup whilst having a bath first, that way dribbles don't matter.

* If food needs cooling down quickly - add an ice cube, or some of your frozen food cubes.

* Don't start mixed feeding if baby is hungry, teething or tired - s/he will just scream.

* **Never re-use food** that has had an eating spoon in it - saliva on the spoon can then break down the food and cause it to decay.

* Do not **sweeten** food and don't use sweetened commercial food - your baby will develop a sweet tooth. Do not add salt either.

* Full strength **cow's milk** is best not given until a baby is twelve months old. Even then, I'd boil it at first.

* Never leave baby alone when eating in case of choking.

* Give no egg white until one year old.

* **Never reheat** food for your baby as there is a chance of infection.

* Give no **gluten** or **cereal** until your baby is at least six months old.

* Do not add cereal to the milk. It prevents the calcium in milk being used effectively - and can lead to obesity.

* Do not let cereals constitute a large part of the meal.

* Try not to transmit your own personal dislikes of food, by facial expression or your tone of voice. Be enthusiastic and encourage varied tastes.

Suggested Meals

Breakfasts	Ground rice plus puréed fruit - apple, pear, bananas, apricot. As baby gets older, wholemeal bread with peanut butter, cereal or porridge.
Dinners	Vegetables - puréed carrots, parsnips, potatoes; later add white fish, haddock, cod, then chicken, poached and puréed.
Teas	Avocado and banana, puréed. Cottage cheese and apple purée. Later boiled egg, bread and butter.
Puddings	Purée fruits and yoghurts, ice creams.
Snacks (later)	Rice cakes, raw carrots, fruit, raisins.

Teething
and teeth care

Babies can teethe at any time, some are even born with teeth. Others do not get any until their first birthday. This is all normal but just to give you a general idea of what to expect, here are a few averages.

* The approximate age for the **first tooth** to appear is six months.

* The first teeth to appear are usually the **bottom front**, the second following the first quite quickly.

* The tooth is visible as a pale, hard bump just below the surface, then its sharp pointed edge breaks through. The first few teeth tend to give only a little trouble.

* The ones that give a lot of trouble are the **side molars**, as they are bigger and flatter. They tend to come up at around a year.

* Signs and symptoms to expect are **inflamed gums**, lots of **dribbling** and **chewing**, slight crankiness, nappies may be looser than usual so change more regularly. It is a prime time for sore bottoms to occur and maybe fretfulness.

* Teething does not cause fever, vomiting, loss of appetite or fits. If your baby is suffering from these symptoms s/he is ill and should be taken to a doctor.

Teething tips   * Teething babies need lots of tender loving care; they don't understand why they feel this way.

      * Teething is a difficult time to cope with, make sure you get time to relax away from your teething baby. There are plenty of medicines to help, but it is best to give teething gels or homoeopathic remedies in the day time, except when real pain is obvious, for example, with the molar teeth. Medication may make baby sleepy and even more irritable. Restrict the use of sedation or pain killing teething medications to night time, and use with extreme care. The homoeopathic remedy, which is very soothing, is in granular or drop form and called Chamomilla 2x (available by post too - details at the back of this book).

* Start introducing **hard food** like pieces of apple, carrot and crusts - baked in an oven to harden. I find hard baked pitta bread a godsend.

* Other **teething aids** - a frozen banana, cut lengthwise. A frozen roll, frozen water-filled teething rings, an ice cube tied in a clean flannel with string, a clean rubber ring.

* If you want your child to have healthy teeth, be very careful about avoiding **sweet** drinks and food. If your child needs medicine - try to find a low sugar one.

* Babies should be given hard foods as soon as they start to chew on their toys, but never give these while baby is lying down. Be very watchful even when babies are sitting, as small pieces of food can break off and choke a child. If necessary, a quick pat between the shoulder blades should dislodge food or help baby cough it out.

* In cold weather wrap your baby up cosily in a scarf and hat, especially around the facial teething area.

* Give **cold drinks** frequently to dilute acidity.

* **Clean** your infant's teeth with a small gauze pad, massage over the teeth and gums to remove food debris and plaque. Start with even the first tooth.

* As they get older, start a routine of **brushing teeth** together, morning and evening and after snacks if possible. Make it fun, let them pick a present of a new toothbrush. Let them clean their teeth in the bath and make a dribbly mess. Always give a good example and clean your own teeth regularly.

* Take your child to the **dentist** on your own appointment at about eighteen months and perhaps introduce the idea of a tooth doctor.

* **Dental plaque** is the major cause of tooth decay and gum disease today, to remove it, we need to brush our teeth at least twice a day.

* Brushing your teeth, be consistent and thorough, starting at front brushing the inside and outside surfaces, then going to the back teeth again, doing the outside and inside surfaces thoroughly.

* Use a good **tooth brush** and change it at least every three months.

* As your children get older, ask your dentist to teach them how to brush their teeth. Children under six need help and lots of encouragement to brush their teeth and develop a good brushing technique.

* Many dentists advise a fluoride **mouth wash** for children (over six) in areas where there is no fluoride added to the drinking water as it strengthens the outer surface and prevents tooth decay.

* Also, to prevent children's molar teeth from decaying your dentist can put a tough plastic coating onto the back teeth. This seals fissures, prevents bacteria and therefore tooth decay. Ask your dentist about this **pit and fissure sealing** treatment. It is best to have each permanent molar and pre-molar tooth treated this way as soon as it has erupted.

Nappy rash

This can range from mild redness to very inflamed skin, with bleeding from broken skin in severe cases. Urine left next to the skin can be broken down by the baby's stools to produce ammonia which is a bad irritant and can burn the skin. Babies with sensitive skins are more prone to nappy rash than others. So if you have a baby with sensitive fair skin, or a family history of allergies, eczema or sensitivities it pays to be extra-vigilant, changing the nappy immediately baby has soiled. But however much you try to avoid it, it is almost certain that your baby will get nappy rash at some stage. A lot of parents feel guilty about this, as if it's a reflection of their caring. This is simply not true; even the most treasured, loved and well cared for babies get nappy rash. Below are tips tried and tested ways of preventing and, if needs be, treating nappy rash.

Tips for preventing nappy rash

* Change nappy as soon as soiled or wet.

* Use a **one way nappy-liner** if you can get one (available through MOTHERCARE - details at the back of this book). Fabric ones are better than disposable.

* Leave the nappy off as much as possible, let the **fresh air** get at baby's bottom.

* Use a **barrier cream**, such as Vaseline or zinc-starch powder.

* Be very careful if using cloth nappies to pay attention to sterilising, washing, and rinsing thoroughly.

* Do not use plastic pants.

* If baby's skin starts to get red, stop washing with soap and water, as it could dry out the skin.

Treating   *   Change nappy more frequently.

Nappy Rash   *   Try other nappies (eg change from terry to disposable or vice versa).

* Stop using **detergents** and **fabric conditioner** on cloth nappies.

* If buying a new **nappy cream,** buy a small pot first to see if it suits.

* Be careful not to clog nappy liners with cream.

* Try using no cream, but just leave nappy off and let the warm air heal - you could dry the baby's bottom with a hair dryer set on cool but be extremely careful not to burn baby's sensitive skin.

* If rash starts around back passage and moves to buttocks it could be **thrush**. Check with your doctor as thrush needs to be treated with prescription cream and medicine.

* Egg white smoothed onto baby's bottom can aid healing beautifully (be sure your baby is not allergic to eggs).

* Try a combination of all these tips but if nappy rash persists or is severe, see your GP who will prescribe something to heal it. *Note*: Occasionally, nappy rash can be the result of **overfeeding.**

* Finally, my preferred bottom care was just **zinc-starch powder,** sometimes with Vaseline to protect, and at the first sign of soreness either add calendula to the Vaseline or use a nappy rash cream.

Crying

It's only when you become a parent that you fully appreciate how disturbing, even heartbreaking, it can be to hear your own baby crying.

Babies' cries are their powerful means of survival. They can make a parent feel desperate and are meant to! Crying is a way of attracting your attention. Let me just say that there is no such thing as a 'good' or 'bad' baby. When people ask whether your baby is 'good' they usually mean 'Does she cry a lot?' or 'Does she sleep well?' Babies cry because they are trying to tell you they want something. For this reason you shouldn't ignore the cries. Crying does not 'exercise the lungs' and it is not 'good for babies' to cry excessively or for long periods. Also, if your baby does cry a lot, it does not make you a 'bad' parent either. Babies who cry constantly are enough to try the patience of a saint. So let's find out what we can do about it.

Reasons for crying - a check-list

* **Wanting to be near you.** Having been inside you for nine months, young babies in particular may crave the comfort of having you near.

* **Hunger.** Try a feed and see. You can generally tell if babies are getting enough milk by counting their wet nappies, six to eight daily is an average guide.

* **Thirst.**

* **Wind** or **colic pain.** This may occur as a result of over-feeding, underfeeding, allergy (often a reaction to cow's milk), over-anxious parents or excessive bowel action. Evening colic can be caused by wind pain from an excessive morning feed eight to twelve hours earlier.

* **Discomfort** - being too hot or too cold; hands, feet, fingers or toes may be uncomfortably restrained, ensure clothes are not tight anywhere.

* **Nappy needs changing.** Is baby's bottom dirty, wet or just sore? (See **Nappy Rash** section.)

* **Feeding problems,** for example, maybe the milk isn't coming quickly enough. If breastfeeding, drink plenty, and express to encourage flow. If bottle feeding, check the teat. Make sure you use the correct bottle teat and formula for your baby's age.

* **Boredom.** Being over-tired and restless, but unable to sleep.

* **Reaction to your feelings.** Are you anxious, upset, unhappy?

Cures * **Contact.** Use a sling or carrier to keep baby close. This enables you to carry on with life and still use two hands. A back-carrier makes the weight of even the older baby easier to carry, enabling you to get out and about. It can be liberating and usually stops the crying.

* **Swaddle**, or closely wrap your baby up to give security, even wrap baby to you with a big shawl as they do in Wales. Walk with baby in a pram or buggy or go on a car drive: movement may soothe baby asleep. I've known parents to drive around the block a hundred times for peace!

* Get a break for yourself, to collect yourself and **relax**, taking slow breaths - go for a brisk walk if possible.

* **Sing** to your baby. If you are a hopeless singer, hum, rock and dance to music with your baby in your arms.

* Get a **cassette** of womb noises or just play a cassette to yourself (and baby) during pregnancy (soft or classical to help you both relax) and you'll find that later the baby will recognise it and will relax too with the familiar sounds, even after birth.

* Turning the vacuum cleaner on can help - honestly! A lot of household machines can have a similar effect.

* Some babies love sleeping on **lambswool rugs**.

* Try a **soother** to calm a fractious baby but do restrict its use.

* Babies get bored when they can't see what's going on. Use a baby **lie back chair** or **bouncer**.

* Babies who cry **at night** may be better off beside you in your bed, or move the **cot** beside your bed.

* Check baby's **diet** thoroughly for an allergy (see **Allergies**). If breastfeeding check your own diet.

* Babies who had a difficult birth, or delayed contact with their mother, may be prone to crying a lot. Increased physical contact often helps. **Massage** baby to soothe.

* The herb dill eaten by the mother if breastfeeding often helps a colicky baby. Or chamomile drops can be given directly to the baby.

* **Try gripe water**, but note that babies less than six months must not be given more than 5mls of gripe water at a time, and never more than eight times in a twenty-four hour period. Infant colic drops can be purchased from a chemist.

* **Anti-spasmodic drugs** can be prescribed by your GP.

* If **unusual crying** persists do see your doctor or public health nurse - there could be a physical cause, for example earache or sore throat.

* If you get desperate, put the baby in another room and close the door, and have a calm breather. Phone someone and ask advice, a friend, a teacher from your antenatal class, a breastfeeding counsellor, your partner - share your frustration. If you can't think of anyone phone PARENTS UNDER STRESS (number at the back of this book).

* Some babies cry for no apparent reason. All you can do is accept it and call on all the patience and understanding you can muster. Give plenty of tender loving care - but never forget yourself and your own needs.

Establishing a
good sleeping routine

All people, adults, babies and children, have different sleeping patterns and needs. You are not necessarily a good parent just because your newborn sleeps through the night; neither are you a bad one if your baby does not. In fact it is unusual for newborns to sleep through the night. They usually need regular feeding and changing, but straight away some are more wakeful than others. Society tends to put pressure on new parents, with comments like 'is she good, is she sleeping all night for you yet?' So try not to worry about what other people say or think about your baby's sleeping habits. People often forget just what sleepless nights are like and unknowingly say insensitive things, which can upset you especially if you have been up half the night. I thought all the strange nights and shifts I'd done as a nurse would have prepared me for the lack of sleep, but no! Sheer exhaustion can be overwhelming at times, it tends to come upon you at around the five month stage. So be prepared to get sleep where and when you can during the early months. Creating the right environment to encourage your baby to sleep is important, showing baby that there is a difference between day and night from the very beginning is vital. The amount of sleep each baby needs varies tremendously, but if you are ever concerned your baby is not getting enough sleep or is crying too much ask your doctor's advice.

Some of these tips on establishing a routine would not suit every parent. Just work down the list and pick the ones you think may suit you and your little one. And do remember, one in three children wakes up regularly in the night at twelve months old.

Tips on establishing a sleeping routine

* Get into a night time routine and try and stick to it. For example, evening bath and feed at 6:00 pm, followed by a feed as you are going to bed around 10:00pm.

* Some parents like to take the baby to bed with them, and so long as it suits everyone it can be a great solution.

* Others keep the cradle in their bedroom for the first two to three months until the night feedings are less frequent.

* Some parents keep their babies in a separate bedroom from the first night then, once established, the sleeping routine can be continued without the disturbance of changing rooms.

* **Right from the beginning certain things will encourage your baby to sleep, so be careful you do not initiate a pattern you are not going to want to keep up.**

* If you can teach your baby to sleep without needing to suckle or have a bottle it is a good idea to do so. This way your baby is less likely to disturb you if s/he wakes during the night.

* Start as you mean to go on - make night time feeding undesirable for the baby. For example, make it boring, feed in a darkened room, avoid noise, do not play. In the day time give lots of playtime attention but not at night.

* Avoid unnecessary **light, noise** and **movement** at night - use a night light.

* Avoid changing nappies at night unless baby has passed a motion.

* There are many devices that are supposed to encourage babies to sleep and some do work, but they should be started from the very beginning, from before two months old.

* **Tape recordings** of gentle music played whilst baby was relaxing in your womb could be continued.

* All babies make sounds and little cries through the night. They have different sleep levels to ours, rousing slightly nearly every hour. So babies may wake a few times during the night, resist the urge to go to them and they may just settle down again. Of course, if your baby genuinely needs you the cries will become loud and demanding and you should attend to them.

* Never leave babies crying too long, this may make them feel insecure .

* Try to have a day time pattern which includes a **rest period** for mother in the morning so she can catch up on any missed sleep.

* Take any help you can get if you are tired. Let relatives, friends and neighbours take the baby for a while so you can sleep and don't feel guilty about it. Sleep is a priority - a happy rested parent is most important.

* At around three to six months a **sleeping pattern** hopefully will start to emerge. Baby will start to recognise the difference between night and day.

* If this is not the case, keep a record of your baby's wakings and see if you can identify reasons for wakings.

* Once a baby gets to three to six months old and is putting on weight and taking good day time feeds, night time feeds are not necessary but may have been turned into a habit. Keep trying to make these as boring and low key

as possible, slowly lessening the amount given and hopefully the need for them will gradually diminish.

* In winter the **cold** can wake a baby up so keep the temperature constant if possible, or use a thick sleep suit in case baby kicks bedclothes off at night.

* Try giving your child a little relaxing **massage** before bedtime, after reading a story.

* Teach your children **relaxation techniques,** relaxing all their muscles one by one, starting with the toes.

* Play the game of picking a dream to have as they go asleep, 'are you being Cinderella tonight?'

* Encourage a **comfort toy** that is taken to bed every night to give security.

Sleeping problems

When one of your children has a sleeping problem the world can seem as if it's coming to an end. You're probably so tired you don't even know how to begin to tackle the problem. You may feel at your wit's end but let me assure you here and now that there are ways of dealing with almost all of these problems. The best way of tackling sleeping problems is to be firm and consistent, using techniques that are fair and adapted to suit your own child's particular needs. Tackle the problem confidently, a child can pick out half-hearted, weak attempts before they even start, so be positive. Go forward womanly or manly together where many parents have bravely gone before, to find out who really rules the night!

Common reasons for sleep problems and possible solutions

* Is your baby getting **overtired**? Contrary to popular belief keeping babies from napping can make them so overtired they may become more difficult to settle down, not less.

* **Noise** on a constant basis may be comforting to babies, but sudden noises may waken them. For example, dogs barking, a train going past. Check this out.

* **Wind** can be caused by the wrong teat, or wrong size of hole in teat, by a profusion of breast milk, by mother eating high fibre foods or by simply not getting all the wind up.

* **Colic** is most distressing for both baby and parents. Symptoms include excessive screaming and cramps. Babies often outgrow it naturally around three months. Colic drops given to the baby or the herb dill taken by the breastfeeding mother may help (see additional reading list).

* **Hyperactive children** who do not seem to need much sleep may benefit from having their diet completely revised. They may be sensitive to certain foods, such as cow's milk, dairy products and foods containing artificial preservatives and colorants. Foods containing E102 especially can cause wakefulness.

* Is it testing time? Sometimes children - especially around two years of age - test you to see how far they can go. **Be firm.**

* Make sure there is nothing **frightening** in the room, use a night light, change the room around, ask children are they frightened of something.

* Something **new** in the room could encourage your child to stay in bed, for example, a new poster, or bedspread or cuddly toy.

* For older children try a **reward or star** chart for going to bed on time or not getting up in the night.

Other ideas * If a child who normally sleeps through the night suddenly starts waking, it may indicate a **health problem**, for example earache, which is very common in toddlers in winter time, or eczema, which is associated with allergies. A visit to your GP may be worthwhile.

* Inconsistent sleeping routines can cause problems - see previous tips on **Establishing a sleeping routine.**

* **Anxiety** causes wakefulness - talk to your children and reassure them.

* Leave a **drink** or a **nibble** by the bedside if your child regularly wakes feeling hungry or thirsty. Leave it as you go to bed, or it will be eaten too soon. If your child wants you to stay in the room, develop a routine that slowly gets you out of the room. For example, sit at the bedside the first night, move to the bottom of the bed the following night, gradually move to the door, then stay outside the door.

* **Milky drinks** contain calcium, nature's tranquilliser, so give a milky drink before bed.

* Don't change from activities to bedtime too quickly, allow time to **unwind.**

Early wakers * Ensure they get plenty of **fresh air** and **exercise** in the day time.

* Try a later bedtime.

* Give a **book** or **toys** to keep in the cot or bed to keep them occupied in the morning so they will not disturb you.

* Food and drink can be left as you go to bed for a morning snack.

* Try the **reward charts.** If you are not disturbed until the alarm goes off or until the clock says 7:00 am a star is given.

A last resort
- the
checking
ritual

* If your child wakes and starts to cry, go in and reassure her/him and check that nothing is wrong.

* Be firm and deliberate; show you are not going to pick her/him up. Talk to your child, say that it is sleep time, settle the child and leave the room.

* If the crying continues wait for five minutes, then go back in. Do not speak this time, just settle the child down, ensure all is OK and come out.

* If crying still continues, this time wait ten minutes before going back in, settle child down and come out.

* Continue checking, as necessary, every fifteen minutes until s/he falls asleep.

* If your child wakes simply out of habit, gradually lengthen the last waiting time to twenty minutes.

* Eventually your child will get the message that waking will not do them any good.

* For the checking ritual to work you must be consistent, firm and have the support of your partner. It is very difficult not to give in when your child is screaming.

* Remember the goal is to teach your child to have a good healthy sleep pattern. A child deprived of sleep is not healthy, so your child will benefit in the long run.

* Remember the checking ritual is only used when all other avenues have been tried. It's not good for children to be left crying if they are in need of anything.

Other hints

* Don't both of you get exhausted - take turns sleeping and checking.

* Take any help or support you can get if it gives you sleep or some sort of relief.

* Eat well, it's no time to be dieting. You need lots of strength. Take a course of multi-vitamins and minerals or a course of royal jelly as a pick-me-up.

* Start a diary to see any improvement, make a list of priorities and jobs to be done. Sleeplessness can make you very forgetful.

* Talk to other parents for any other tips.

* During this tiring stage do not expect too much of yourself, parties may be out for a while. Do the minimum you can get away with and be kind to yourself.

Night Terrors

Night terrors can consist of children partially waking, screaming, and hysterically thrashing themselves around the bed and maybe even sleepwalking. These terrors occur when the child is going from a deep sleep to a lighter sleep and is having difficulty going from one stage to the other. This can happen when children are undergoing changes in their lives or as a result of tension, for example starting school or family disharmony. However, around the ages of five to eight, they can be due to purely developmental reasons. There is a definite difference between nightmares and night terrors, usually the terrors are physiological and the child remembers nothing. On the other hand, nightmares may be remembered and if associated with other symptoms like bed wetting can be a sign of stress. I can reassure parents that these terrors do not harm the child in any way.

Tips for dealing with night terrors

* The best solution is to completely ignore these night terrors and only respond if the child asks to be held or protected. It is difficult to ignore but this phase will pass naturally itself.

* Another idea is to partially wake the child one hour prior to the time the terror usually occurs. This tends to work very well as it helps the child to make the transition from deep to light sleep.

* Check is anything in your child's life causing unease, and correct it if possible.

* Partial wakings, sleep walking and night terrors in older children and teenagers tend to be caused by emotional or psychological problems and these must be investigated.

* If a child does sleep walk the parents must make the house 'walk-proof', for example keep a night light on in the landing, lock all windows, put high locks on doors, remove toys or obstacles that may be tripped over prior to bedtime.

Potty training

Potty training can cause parents a lot of anguish, and yet it shouldn't if you put it in the right perspective. For example, about fifty years ago it was common for parents to try to potty train at six months. You can imagine the problems that caused. There is no point in beginning toilet training until your child's muscles and nerves are sufficiently developed. The necessary stage of development does not occur until around age two and sometimes later. With this in mind the key to successful hassle-free potty training is **start late, stay cool and accept mistakes**.

To be ready for toilet training children need:

* To have a dry nappy for a reasonable length of time (two hours) or at the afternoon nap time.

* To be capable of letting you know when they want to go, by words, gestures or facial movements.

* To be able to sit comfortably on a potty or, for boys, stand steadily without support.

* To understand the words for going to the toilet (wee wee, poo poo or whatever names you use).

* To be able to remove their own pants.

* To be happy, settled and secure.

* To understand the whole procedure - talk about it!

To train your child, you need:

* To be in the right mood.

* To feel intuitively that the time is right.

* To be free from other worries. You need to stay calm, accept little accidents.

* To have time to give to training.

Practical tips

* Buy a potty - let your child choose it or put a special name on it or liven it up with a big red bow - **be positive** and make it a treat. It could be a birthday present to mark the second birthday.

* Explain what it's for. Older children can give an example here and parents can also explain by showing.

* Decide to have a few **positive training days.** Stay at home mostly during this week otherwise you'll have problems when you go visiting etc.

* Start by encouraging your child to sit on the potty.

* Then make it a **routine** to sit on the potty first thing in the morning, after meals, and before bed.

* Be encouraging. Be pleased even when they just sit on the potty, and even more if they actually use the potty (don't overdo it though).

* Encourage them to look for the potty themselves and have it in view or bring it to view hourly as a reminder that it is available.

* If your child regularly opens her/his bowels after breakfast (to do 'poo poo') put her/him on the potty at this regular time.

* **Leave the nappies off** whilst having training times and keep the potty at hand. If it's summer let your child run round the garden with no panties on.

* Eventually you'll be able to abandon nappies altogether - use **trainer pants** at this stage if you like but the odd flood is inevitable.

* Always keep the potty accessible, sit your child on it hourly if necessary.

* Use clothes that are easily pulled down and up and easily washed too.

* Later show how to use **the toilet,** a step can be used. Show how to use toilet paper and how to wash hands, then pull the chain - start good toilet habits now.

* At around three to four when your child has had dry nappies in the morning for a few nights or fairly regularly you could leave the nappy off. But protect the mattress. Watch fluid intake after 6:00pm and encourage using the potty just before bed. See **Becoming dry at night.**

Got a problem?

* **Be flexible**: rigid rules hinder rather than help.

* You may have **started too early**. What's the rush? Leave it for a week or so and start again and repeat if necessary. Your child will do it when s/he's able.

* Do be prepared for **accidents**, have a spare potty in the car, take a change of clothes when you go out. Don't make a fuss. Keep a bucket of water with diluted disinfectant handy for mop ups.

* Don't compare or compete with other parents or children.

* If a genuine problem occurs seek advice from a public health nurse, GP, or a friend.

* Getting a child trained early is not a sign of high intelligence in the parent or the child. Let your child determine the pace.

* Always remember that praising and rewarding efforts works better than scolding the unwanted behaviour. Give them a **positive attitude** to their body and its necessary functions.

* **Good luck**. I know it can be trying at times, but try to make it a fun game.

Becoming dry
at night

As with potty training, children tend to learn night time bladder control at their own pace. Parents who are relaxed and encouraging tend to get quicker results. Also very few children are aware that they are wetting the bed so scolding is not the answer. It only leads to extra anxiety which tends to make the problem worse. All we parents can do is help through guidance and encouragement. Begin around the age of three or four. If your child has been dry in the day for a couple of months and is comfortable with that and the nappy has been dry for a couple of mornings you could find out simply by asking 'Would you like to try and come out of nappies at night time too?' If the answer is yes, just take the nappy off, but protect the mattress. The speed at which children achieve night time control varies tremendously. You may start only with two dry nights out of the first week, gradually improving to three or four over the following weeks. This is progress! Praise the dry nights, don't show too much disappointment on the wet mornings. If constant bed-wetting occurs try again in two to three months, your child may just not be ready yet.

Tips on becoming dry at night

* Develop a **night time routine** to encourage dryness. Cut down on fluids after 6:00pm, if you do give an early evening drink avoid tea, coffee and fizzy drinks as these encourage the body to produce more urine. Do ensure, though, that your little one gets plenty of fluid throughout the day. Six cups are recommended.

* Visit the **toilet** last thing at night and fully empty bladder. You could even say 'is that the last drop, try - any more? Good!'

* Leave the potty beside the bed at first, especially if the toilet is a distance away.

* Leave the bedroom **night light** or landing light on.

* Make sure the bedroom is warm enough.

* If using bunk beds always give the bottom one to the child being toilet-trained. It is safer anyway.

* Prevent your child from becoming **constipated** at this time because a full bowel can tend to 'irritate' the bladder. Give a diet with plenty of roughage.

* You could try the **lifting technique** at first to reduce the number of wet beds and laundry. It simply means when you go to bed later in the night lift your child onto the potty or toilet - let them waken a bit, so they learn the sensation of a full bladder.

* Do the lifting technique even if the bed is already wet - it pays to still encourage urination (wee wee).

* Gradually stop the night time lifting after a couple of weeks or months as necessary.

If your child
is over five
years old and
is still not
dry

* A lot of children do still wet the bed at five years old - there's nothing wrong with them. It is difficult to know what causes it. It's as if they don't get tuned in to their body's sensations until at a later age but we can help.

* Firstly make sure you have already tried the steps mentioned above.

* If your little one has smelly urine, difficulty or pain on passing water, soreness in the genital area, or is frequently thirsty or still wet day and night - go and chat about the whole thing with your GP. An infection may be the cause.

* Bed wetting does have a familial tendency.

* Life changes such as a new baby, a death in the family, starting a different school or moving house can delay control and start bed wetting.

* In each classroom there is likely to be one or two children with a bed wetting problem. It tends to be more common in boys than in girls.

* **Praise** always works wonders! Praise the dry nights, or even attempts to get to the toilet. Try not to let frustration show when you see yet another wet bed.

* Reward. **Star charts** can help. Design one of your own. Choose what the reward will be for dry bed, or for any small wet patches. Stick stars on to the grid of the chart. For example, for three stars award with a treat or small toy. Use whatever suits your individual child, but make it an incentive to succeed.

* Draw a dot-to-dot picture of your child's favourite toy. Join two dots for a dry bed and when the picture is complete, a big reward is in store.

If your child is over seven years old and still not dry

* If you have not visited your GP yet now is the time to go for that chat.

* At this stage your child may be getting anxious about it too. Talk together calmly about the problem. It may uncover a fear or anxiety. Be open and listen.

* Talk generally about how everybody has problems with performing certain functions. Some need to wear spectacles. Some are good at swimming, others not. Reassure.

* Your child needs to be motivated and must really want to become dry at night. Discuss, gently, some of the good reasons for being dry at night.

* Children need to feel in control of their bladders - start by getting them to say out loud 'I want to be dry, I'm in charge of my bladder.' Repeat a few times daily.

* Exercises may help. A child can sing a nursery rhyme or count to ten, just holding on a little longer before going to the toilet. This muscle control in the day may improve muscle control at night.

* Self-waking may help the older child to feel in control. Teach how to set an alarm clock at certain times, for example around 2:00 am or two hours before normal waking time, or just before the time wetting seems to occur.

* Do talk it over with a professional who may be able to help, for example, a social worker, health nurse, GP, school nurse. They will be able to reassure and also they may see a problem you may be overlooking. Also contact ERIC, the ENURESIS INFORMATION CENTRE (their address is at the back of this book).

Tips on buzzers and bedwetting alarms

* There are basically two types of bedwetting alarms. Bedside alarms have two detector mats placed under the sheet and a noise box next to the bed. The second type consists of a very small noise box and detector near the child in the bed. Both types buzz or ring when wet, and waken the child, hopefully enabling them to hold on and gradually learn the sensation of a full bladder and thus achieve bladder control. In the UK they can be obtained on loan from the National Health Service. In Ireland ask the Public Health Nurse or GP for advice. They can also be purchased (see addresses for supplier).

* Medicine can be prescribed by your GP but should only be used for short periods, for example while visiting or on holidays. Some medicines may have unpleasant side effects - ask your GP about this.

* It is well worth investing in a plastic sheet or mattress cover.

* If having day time and night accidents, it is very important to know where the toilets are and have easy access to one at all times. An easy clothes change in a bag may be a good idea. A quiet confidential word with the school teacher is a *must* - do enlist sympathetic adults' support.

Tips if using an alarm

* It may be easier to leave off pyjama bottoms.

* Your child must routinely switch on alarm before sleeping.

* Have the alarm situated so the child must get out of bed to switch it off, or else they may just roll over and go back to sleep.

* Note the size and time of wet patch nightly, noting improvements.

* Ensure your child finishes the urination in the toilet before going back to sleep.

* Put out a spare sheet, nightie etc beside the bed for changing.

* Switch alarm back on if accident occurs.

* In the morning, switch off alarm and fill in record chart.

* Ensure your child knows exactly what the alarm is for and how it is supposed to work.

* All these suggestions may take months to work. Be encouraging, persevere even though it can get very frustrating at times. It can be a very demanding, difficult problem for parents. Share your frustration with a sympathetic friend, or away from your family give out a good yell! It always makes you feel better afterwards.

* For useful books and organisations see the back of this book.

Speech

Children learn to talk and in fact do all sorts of things at different rates. Some are slower at talking, others walking. Here are a few guidelines and practical tips on what to expect and what to do if something is worrying you about your child's speech development. But do keep worries in perspective, minor speech difficulties in early years can be completely overcome with a little help. It is never any harm to investigate suspected difficulties, as language and communication skills are very important for our children's development as social beings. Encourage speech by talking to your baby; describe, sing lullabies, repeat nursery rhymes and play games like 'This little piggy'. Explain what you are doing all the time. 'I'm changing your nappy', 'Let's open the door and go down the stairs'. Use books with your baby from very early on. Then listen while they practice their sounds, show how interested you are in hearing them speak, even if you can't understand a word. Look out for books like *Round and Round the Garden* by Sarah Williams (Oxford Press) that combine sight, sound, rhyme, actions and words.

What you can expect

* By **one year old,** babies are making lovely sounds babbling and perhaps a few simple words like 'bye, bye'.

* **Between one and two years,** they can speak their first words and understand a lot more.

* At **two,** the words start to be put together. 'All gone' 'Mummy work', 'Rory school'.

* By **three,** you can expect four and five word sentences and your child's vocabulary in this year grows rapidly. Also the endings of words will be correct, for example 'I am playing / I played' and the child will discover words like 'the', 'it', 'on', 'and'.

* At **four,** they should understand nearly everything you say and know thousands of words, though they will still make mistakes.

Common worries and problems

* **Late talkers:** if your child is not making noises by one year or not talking by two get your GP to refer you to a speech therapist.

* Get your GP to check **hearing.** A glue ear, repeated ear infections, colds or measles can affect hearing which in turn can affect speech.

* As a general guide, you should seek help if your child can't follow simple instructions by age two and-a-half years; or if other people can't understand your child's speech by about four years; or if speech is still or halting by five years.

* Be sure you are stimulating your child enough, **speak, listen, read,** point out **names** of objects.

* One in three children stumble or stammer on their speech at first - it usually resolves itself.

* **Don't tease,** speak for, or correct your child and don't show concern - it should pass.

* Seek help if the stammer gets worse, if anyone else in the family stammers, if it is affecting relationships, or just continues and shows no sign of disappearing by about age five.

* Virtually all children have pronunciation problems at some stage. Be careful not to correct constantly, it makes a child tense and self-conscious.

* Seek help if you find it difficult to interpret your child's speech by about three years, or if pronunciation deteriorates, or if s/he is five years old and still having problems.

* **Don't delay:** If it is a real speech problem, it's vital that it's picked up early or it can cause behavioural or learning difficulties. It may also cause problems in relationships and may affect confidence. If in doubt then check it out, go to your GP or speech therapist, (useful addresses given at the back of this book).

Food hints
and recipes

The more I read about health and diet, the more I realise the importance of giving our children a good start in life by giving them **good eating habits** from a very early age. I know it is difficult to get them not to eat sweets and almost impossible to get them to eat the vegetables and salads that we would love them to eat. Do not despair. Here are a few facts that may comfort you.

All bread, be it white or brown is nutritious; white and brown bread differ only in fibre content, so if they will not eat wholemeal bread try partly wholemeal, or bread containing oats which also has fibre. Get the fibre another way, for example from beans, pulses, fresh fruit, vegetables or breakfast cereals. If your child is a faddy eater, don't be afraid of just giving **nutritious snacks** on a regular basis instead of big meals. Convenience foods are not *all* bad and frozen or tinned foods can be even better than fresh that has been stored badly. But do ensure you do not buy any tins that have dents or bulging tops. If you can, preserve the fibre by giving foods such as potatoes, carrots, and apples with their skins washed but intact.

Offer your children a **wide range of foods**. They tend to be open to all types of foods during their pre-school years so experiment a little. The secret is to only buy the foods that you would really like your children to eat. Try not to give sweets as a reward for good behaviour. If you do give sweets restrict them to after meals to minimise the damage to their teeth. Or try having just one day a week when they are allowed sweets and brush their teeth well that night. I must say I quite often give sweets, not the coloured ones but the chocolate type, after meals instead of puddings.

Finally if your children are on a **special diet** or you prefer them not to eat certain foods, do inform relatives and friends who are likely to arrive with bags of goodies for them (with the best will in the world) and do let them know what alternatives they can bring as a present. Also watch out for children's parties and if necessary pack their own goodies in a bag so they can bring them and feel they are still sharing in the fun.

Remember that eating healthily does not have to mean hard work. Take a look at some of the nutritious snacks and recipes on the following pages. I have kept them simple, quick and easy so you can gradually teach your children how to cook them for themselves. This helps children to appreciate how much goes into cooking and they'll appreciate what you do for them more.

Some useful hints and recipes

* Prior to having your baby get your **freezer** stocked up, use ready-made pastry for quick quiches or vol-au-vents. Make up a few containers with basic mince, chicken and fish recipes to add to rice, pasta, and potatoes. Use your supermarket for ice cream, frozen foods, partly baked breads (the garlic breads are a favourite in our house). Before freezing, label containers well so others can do the baking for you.

* When weaning a baby who eats only small amounts, make up large batches and freeze the extra in an ice cube tray or freezer bags. Then thaw as necessary.

* When feeding, use plastic moulded bibs to catch spills. And use plates with suction holders to prevent spills or use a soap suction pad.

* Only fill a child's glass half-full at first for obvious reasons.

* Use an ice cube to cool your baby's food down quickly if you are in a rush.

* Fill an ice cream cone with snacks for a mobile lunch, for example egg mayonnaise, cottage cheese, tuna mix.

* Teach children to eat for themselves at a very early age. Let them help themselves to the snack tray in the fridge, consisting of ham slices, cheese, yoghurt, and prepare a few nice salads in tubs ready for eating.

* Teach them to **cook** with you at an early age, baking cakes, pizza, making sandwiches - teach them to be self-sufficient. Make it fun!

* For **snacks**, give broken nuts or seeds, fruit, cheese, dried fruit, raisins, wholegrain crackers with cheese spread, cottage cheese, peanut butter or marmite, low sugar muesli bars, rice cakes, boiled eggs, carob bars and unsalted crisps. Be careful with nuts as they can choke a child. Do not give them to children under three and never leave a young child eating nuts alone.

* For **drinks** give diluted pure fruit juices or milk.

* Make your own ice pops from fruit juices.

Lunch box ideas

* Fill a pocket-sized **pitta bread** with a mix of tuna fish, and Thousand Island dressing or tomatoes/egg mayonnaise and lettuce or chicken and sweetcorn mixed with their favourite dressing. Also include a small box of raisins and a carton of apple juice.

* Make **wholemeal sandwiches** with corned beef, lettuce and tomatoes or cream cheese and grated apple and carrot mixture or peanut butter. Add milk and a tub of dried fruit.

* **White bread** (the type you can buy containing extra goodness) with jam (the old favourite); fine cheese and ham slices; yeast or vegetable pâté with fine slices of avocado or apple; tropical fruit juice or water, and a yoghurt with a piece of fresh fruit.

* For a change make a few different tubs of **salad**: bean, apple and raisin salad; coleslaw, pineapple and cucumber salad; carrot and pineapple salad; rice and kidney bean salad; potato, salami and olive salad. Add different mayonnaise or french dressings, and put in different sorts of crackers. Add a carob bar and orange juice.

* Other ideas for **sandwiches** include: diced chicken with halved seedless grapes, with mayonnaise and a little tahini; grated apple, carrot and cheese; prawns and thinly sliced avocado and lemon tangy mayonnaise; banana mashed with soft cheese, chopped dates with a dash of lemon; marmite soft cheese and cress (easy on the marmite); humus and pitta bread.

Snack ideas * Here are a few handy **recipes** my children enjoyed, which is very important. There's nothing worse than cooking a meal that is just pushed aside.

* **Stuffed Cheese Potato Bake:** Bake potatoes in a hot oven. When soft, scoop out the middle and add it to the cheese and butter. Put the mix back in and put a little cheese on the top. You can add sweetcorn, mushrooms, bacon bits, or anything you like to taste.

* **Vegetable Bake:** Use any cooked and diced vegetables, for example carrots, potatoes, courgettes, and onions. You also need milk, eggs and grated cheese. Beat the eggs and add milk (4 ozs milk for each egg). Put the mixture, with the vegetables, into an oven dish and sprinkle with cheese. Bake for 15 mins. at 200C or Gas mark 6.

* **Pizza Type Toast.** You need two slices of whole bread, a tomato, a little grated cheese, and two mushrooms. Toast the bread slightly, skin the tomato (place in hot water first) chop it well and spread it on the toast, put on the grated cheese followed by the sliced mushrooms and grill the lot.

Sweet ideas * **Apple Snow.** You need sweet eating apples and egg white (two apples to 1 egg white). Core and peel apples then simmer them in a little water. Purée and allow to cool. Whisk the egg white, then fold into apple mixture.

* Make **fruit cocktail**: with any fresh fruit your children like. For example, pineapple, banana, orange and raisins or even coconut - then it becomes a real tropical cocktail!

* **Eggless cake:** You need 12ozs plain flour, 6ozs margarine, 6ozs brown sugar, 1 teaspoon bread soda, a half pint of cold apple purée, 4ozs chopped dates (or other soaked dried fruit, I like apricots) 4ozs chopped nuts, 2-3 tablespoons of milk or milk substitute, 8ozs of raisins. Rub the flour and margarine together, add dry ingredients, then the fluids. Put the whole mixture into a greased tin (two pound size) Cook for one to one and a half hours at 180C (Gas Mark 4).

* **Peanut Butter Biscuits:** you need 2ozs peanut butter, 3ozs margarine, 5ozs white flour, 4ozs brown sugar and milk (or milk substitute). Mix together the margarine and sugar, then add the peanut butter and flour and add enough milk to make a good consistency. Cut out into any shapes your children desire and cook for 15 minutes at 180C (Gas Mark 4) and allow to cool before they are gobbled up.

* You can buy lovely books on how to make beautiful **cakes.** But if you are lazy (like me) great things can be done with a large tub of ice cream turned upside down and decorated as a house, train or car, using chocolate buttons, flakes and different sweets. Bought cakes and Swiss rolls can be made into all sorts of robots, and automobiles, so if you don't have time to cook, at least be inventive. I just serve the ice cream cake in cones with the goodies on top.

* When buying food let your motto be 'the fresher the better'. Grow your own fruit and vegetables wherever possible.

* Buy **organically grown** food if you possibly can. I know it tends to be more expensive but remember most of the goodness is in the skin of the vegetables and so are most of the pesticides.

* Take care with the **storage** of food at home: the longer you store it the more the goodness is lost. Maintain safe fridge temperatures (0-3 degrees centigrade), keep raw and cooked foods rigidly apart.

* Buy small amounts of **vegetables**, rather than in big
  quantities. Store them in a cool, dark place for no longer
  than three days. Don't soak before cooking. Steaming and
  microwaving, where little water is used, are the best
  cooking methods.

* **Yoghurt** can aid digestive disorders, thrush, and many
  other minor ailments. Eat the active types, with high
  levels of bacteria. Yoghurt is particularly helpful if you
  have been on a course of antibiotics.

* Finally, it may seem too big a job to switch to a healthy,
  wholesome diet if your children have already developed
  bad habits, but it need not be. Take them shopping with
  you, explain about additives and what they are doing to
  the foods and the environment by adding all these
  chemicals to the food we eat. Get them interested, let
  them look at the labels, explain why you are doing it all,
  and surprisingly they may turn out to be healthier eaters
  than you in the end.

Facts of life

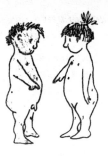

In recent surveys in Ireland and the UK most parents wanted their children to receive some sort of education about sexual matters and bodily functions. I agree wholeheartedly and have done some talks on the subject myself. But really, we parents are our children's first natural teachers and I believe that matters of a personal nature should be discussed not only in group form in a class-room but also in one-to-one situations, with someone who we know loves and cares for us.

All life should be one long, open learning process, things should be talked about openly as they come along. There are so many opportunities for us to share and talk about our feelings on a day to day basis. We should seize these opportunities and have an open household where any subject can be discussed. If you get embarrassed about certain sensitive subjects, then openly tell your children you find it difficult to talk about them, but you want to be honest. If you do not know the answer to questions then it is a great opportunity for you to learn together.

Understanding and feeling happy about our own sexuality is so important. A lot of sexual problems come about through lack of knowledge and understanding more than anything else. So let's strive for honest open homes, let's get involved and take an interest if our schools want to teach about the facts of life, but more importantly, let's listen carefully and grasp any opportunity we get to talk about sexual matters in our homes, without asking too many questions of our own. That way we may pave the way for a new healthy attitude to sexuality in our society.

In my list for the facts of life I will ask you to answer some questions too, other times I will just give you something to think about. That way you can really think carefully about your own attitudes to sex and perhaps revise your way of thinking. Sometimes we never stop to question why we feel a certain way about a subject. But if we do not question our own ideas, we may pass on negative attitudes to our children.

Questioning the facts of life

* What questions do you most dread your children asking you?

  Typical questions children ask:

  Should you wait until you are married to have sex?

  How old should you be before you go the whole way?

  What does wanking mean?

  If I touch myself, is it wrong?

  Is it true that some women (or men) have sex with other women (or men). How do they do that, is that wrong?

* Some parents may automatically go on the defensive or be too inquisitive and reply with 'who have you been talking to?' or 'what have you been up to?' or 'what brought this on?' To answer like that would only make your child less likely to ask you in the future. Of course, you may want to know why the question arose, but be thankful that it is you they are asking and not their mates where they may get the wrong answer. Answer as honestly as you can. If you are embarrassed, say so, and explain why. If you are unsure of the answer say that too. Keep it very simple - if they want to go deeper into the subject they'll ask you. Casually, at the end, you could say 'why do you ask?' but probe too much and they may not ask you the next time they have a question.

* In my experience as a mother and a person explaining about bodies and sexuality, if I don't know where to start I always start with myself. That way no one is giggled about or vulnerable but me. You could start by saying 'I remember my first period and how I wasn't sure what to expect,' or 'I remember when I ejaculated for the first time, I was embarrassed and excited but also a little afraid all at the same time.' By using this approach they may open up about themselves, and at any rate it teaches them that it is OK to feel a bit uncertain or to have mixed emotions.

* Just take the opportunities to talk about these subjects as they come up. Don't say, tonight I'll teach her the facts of life. A bit at a time when it seems natural is far easier to do.

* Start with the basics - our bodies. Talk about them with your baby or toddler in the bath. In our home we play the **body game** at bath time starting off with: this is your nose (all touch our noses), then shoulders, heels - three or four different parts of the body (or more) are taught every bath time. The older ones love teaching the young ones. Casually add sexual parts: vagina, penis, nipples, armpits. You name it and just talk about it as casually as the other parts of the body.

* Other opportunities will come up to explain to them why these parts of our bodies are very special. For example, if your little girl insists on playing with her vagina a lot in company, she can be tactfully told how that is a very special part of a girl's or woman's body. Then the next bath time go into the details of why, explain that the vagina is the passageway to where the eggs of new babies are kept. Of course, age dictates the type of language you would use.

* Parents often ask me at **what age** they should start teaching their children the facts of life. As I have said, do it gradually, as opportunities come up. Don't wait to be asked - you could be waiting a long time. We do not wait for them to ask us about what is safe. We just tell them. So don't wait for them to ask about sex or body changes.

* If we do not speak about certain parts of our body or we ignore certain feelings we know we all have, this silence will send very loud messages to our children that it is a taboo subject. This only leads to misunderstandings and makes children uncomfortable with their sexuality. It could also lead to sexual problems in later life.

* Once your children reach the stage where they are having a **story** every night before bedtime why not introduce the story of how a baby is made, or one about the little seed that grows to be a beautiful baby. There are lots of colourful books that make the story highly entertaining for children.

* Once the children know and understand the basic story, opportunities will gradually come for introducing the idea of a bed to get ready for the egg or baby's arrival (periods) and how the seed starts to be produced in the man (wet dreams and ejaculation). These subjects should have been talked about in depth, long before these changes occur, which can be as early as age nine.

* **Understanding** when and why these things will happen to their bodies will prepare children very well. They will not feel odd or strange but comfortable about their bodies and their changes.

* Tell both girls and boys about each other's changes simultaneously. Then the girls will understand the changes happening to the boys in their class too and the same goes for the boys. This will give a mutual respect and understanding during the adolescent years.

* Try to give a **balanced** view on each subject, then give them time and information so they can work issues out for themselves. Try not to just give a one-sided view (yours). They will only come in contact with other views anyway and this will lead to confusion and they may start to distrust you. For example, if you're talking about masturbation you should tell them that opinions differ - some people think it is very wrong to do it, others think it doesn't do anyone any harm, some feel it is totally natural. By all means give your personal view also. Mine is that it is a totally natural way of getting to know your body.

* What about thorny issues like **child abuse** or **incest**? Do children need to know about these things so young? The problem is that with television, radio and the media in general, they most probably will hear about these issues whether you talk about them or not. So it is important they know the truth about such matters. It is a very sad thought that incest and child abuse are happening to so many children right now, and we cannot stop it unless we bring it out into the open, unless we talk about it.

* Regardless of how we feel personally about sexy films, books, videos, soaps on TV, it is important to realise our children will be exposed to all these things. I personally like to discuss these issues openly at home. To help start a discussion I may begin with statements or questions like, 'he has just met her and they are in bed together already, what do you think about that?' Or 'look they have a nude woman on top of a car just to help sell it. I as a woman resent that, what do you feel about it? You don't see nude men thrown on top of cars much, do you?'

* Discussing things in a group can help children to raise sensitive issues. Also give the group the opportunity to write down questions anonymously as they may be too embarrassed to ask.

* Don't be shocked if your innocent eleven year old asks if she should have sex with a boy she likes. Often adolescents may have mistaken ideas about physical closeness - if kissing may happen straight away then why not sex? In many TV programmes, a couple meet, then the next minute are in bed. It is no wonder a child may get confused and need guidance. It is important to discuss sexuality in the context of building relationships, and of course health issues like AIDS.

* Every home should have **books** on this subject for all ages lying around, so the children can read them at their leisure. Also keep others that may be read together on different occasions. Books for the young should have lots of pictures, for older children they should be easy, straight-forward and sympathetic with sensible down-to-earth facts (a selection of useful titles is listed at the back of this book).

* By being **open, honest** and **truthful** about all things you can't go wrong. Don't forget they are bound to giggle sometimes, it's only normal - have a laugh with them. Just because you are talking about sex there is no need to lose your sense of humour.

Child sexual abuse
- Protect your child

It's sad but a range of surveys indicate that approximately between 30% and 45% of children have been sexually assaulted in some way by their eighteenth birthday. The myth that child molesters are strangers is slowly dying. We now know that 85% to 90% of sexually abused children know their abuser. There is no typical offender. Offenders can be men of any age, any profession or background. Some are highly respected members of society - priests, teachers and doctors, or members of the child's family. Many have been abused as children themselves, and statistics show the molesters have usually abused many children before they are actually caught.

So how do we protect our children from this unidentifiable enemy who may pose as a friend, or even be a loved one? Simply warning children not to speak to strangers is not enough. Child sexual abuse is not a pleasant subject and it's very difficult to talk about. There is a myth that it just doesn't happen in 'nice' families or neighbourhoods. Well it does! And before we can begin to tackle it, we must be prepared to look at its reality and strip away the confusion and silence around it. Heightened awareness of the extent and the reality of child abuse has started to happen in the media but we also must bring it down to our everyday lives. We can't pretend it does not happen - it will not just go away.

We cherish children so the subject is especially painful and touchy. But as part of a protection programme for children, we need to teach them about various dangers, including fire, water, roads and abuse. They can learn basic tactics on how to recognise and hopefully avoid attempted abuse, and what to do if they are abused.

Tips on protecting your child

* Always **believe your children** if they tell you someone has touched them. Child abusers may not be strangers, they may be respected members of society, friends or even members of your own family.

* From two to five years old, children have a clear idea of what they like and dislike. Use this.

* Teaching children the names of their various **body parts** is vital if they need to describe where somebody has touched them, and also for teaching them where other people should not touch them.

*   Slowly introduce the idea of good touches and bad touches. For example, punches from bullies are bad, hugs from mum are good.

*   Teach them to trust their instincts. Children can sense something is wrong or that they may be in danger.

*   **Story-telling** or **role-play** can be useful as a basis for talking about what children should do in different situations. For recommended story books see the reading list at the back of this book.

*   Children are taught to respect adults but illustrate by stories or role-playing that their respect for themselves should come first and sometimes children can and should say 'No' to adults.

*   Role-play or stories should never be frightening, only a guide.

*   These 'games' should be a time for lots of questions, so always respond as honestly as you can, without frightening the children.

*   Use the opportunity to talk about possible **solutions** to problems - together work out guidelines for your children.

*   Encourage your children as much as possible to be responsible for their own well-being from an early age.

*   Give them responsibility and tasks - teach them to be independent, so they can make decisions for themselves.

*   Be a **good listener** - children often speak illogically or in riddles or ask the same question over again. Know when you are not recognising their questions satisfactorily. Ask them 'What do you think?' or 'What if?' Draw them out but avoid specific questions which may frighten them or make them withdraw.

*   If a child indicates s/he has been 'touched in a bad way', offer comfort, be understanding, sympathetic and loving, do not be angry or harsh in front of the child as this would only increase their anxiety.

*   Talk gently about what took place, drawing pictures or using dolls if necessary. Try not to show too much horror or too much upset, this can frighten a child.

*   Go for **professional help** if you suspect child abuse.

* Remember that children may let sexual abuse continue because they feel guilty (and never, never is a child at fault in any way) or they are frightened of what will happen if they tell, for example the family splitting up, people going to jail. So be aware of this!

* Do not put your child's name and address or telephone numbers on the outside of schoolbags, or in view.

* Teach your children their name, address and telephone number at an early age.

* Teach children how to answer the telephone, always asking people to identify themselves first before divulging any information, and never telling callers that they are alone.

* Be aware that molesters pick their victims well, but first they must isolate the child. Revise your child's lifestyle and try to avoid unsafe situations.

* When teaching them about their body, explain the special privateness of their penis and vagina. Point out that no one should touch them without their permission.

* Don't force children to kiss grandparents, uncles or anyone else if they don't want to.

* Finally, try to have an open, honest, loving family atmosphere where children can speak freely on any subject and feel safe enough to reveal whatever happens, knowing they will be believed and supported.

* Books helping to teach your child 'how to be safe' and for parents on how to cope with this whole issue are available from the FAMILY PLANNING CLINICS.

Developing
self-worth

Children's self-image is very important for their happiness and fulfilment. A child who believes the world to be a good and happy place, and who feels special and loved has a great advantage over a child who is negative or doubting. Children who have a good image of themselves enjoy challenges, are open and loving and generous towards others. They feel secure within themselves. Parents have a great deal of input into creating their children's self-image.

Building self esteem in our children

* Always **respond** to a baby's distress cry. They cry because they need something and can't talk to tell you. They need to feel safe and secure. It is impossible to spoil a young baby or to give too much love.

* Remember that people are much more important than things. If you are worried the child will break precious things, remove the objects, make your home an enjoyable and safe place.

* Give light at night with a **night light** or open door, it gives them familiar security if they wake up.

* **Diet** is so important. It communicates to children that you love them enough to care about what they eat. You want them to have a healthy life. Caring about what we put into our bodies conveys how we value ourselves.

* Ensure you and your child wear **seat belts** for every car journey. It shows you care about them and as a result they will care about themselves too.

* Treat your children as special and they will beg into believe it. Respect their **uniqueness**, don't compare or criticise, allow them to be themselves.

* Be a good example of a person with a **positive self-image**.

* Give your children lots of opportunities to make decisions for themselves. They need to take on responsibilities from the beginning. We all learn by doing! It develops our confidence. For example, let them choose meals, clothes, care for a pet, do special tasks or grow plants.

* Failing at something does not make you a failure. Teach your children not to fear failure, it comes to us all. We must take risks to grow, we grow from mistakes.

* **Praise** and **encouragement** always work better than negative criticism, or being scolded. Create a home where children are praised for their efforts.

* **Enjoy life** and teach this enjoyment to your children. Be positive, we all have disappointments, but the world's a great place, and people are wonderful.

* Do not tolerate put-downs. 'I can't do that,' 'I'm just no good at ...,' 'I'm too skinny.' Don't give a deep philosophical talk, just respond with positive remarks. 'Of course you can if you try a little more, let's try it together.' 'Skinny? - You're beautiful, better than all those models in the magazines.'

* Never reward annoying behaviour, whining or self-pity with attention. Ignore it as much as you can.

* Encourage **independence**.

* Remember it is the action or the behaviour that is unacceptable, never the child that is bad! Statements like 'You're stupid' 'bad girl' 'You're lazy' ruin a child's self-esteem.

* Give them 'The OK' to be who they are, knowing you'll back them up. And it will give them loads of **confidence**.

* Think about this: Henry Ford once said 'Whether you think you will succeed or not, you are right.'

Listening

What is this life so full of care we don't take the time to stop and stare - or listen. So many arguments would not have been started if we just had listened properly in the first place. How many times have we missed out on what a child or adult was trying to say because we didn't listen closely enough? We hear the birds singing but we don't listen to them. We miss out on so much. I do not mean we have to sit down and listen closely to every sound our children make, but I do think that life gets so busy for parents that sometimes we forget the most important fundamentals. One of them is the ability to listen well.

Listening is a cultivated art and one we need to practise because often people don't come straight out with what they really mean. If we adults sometimes don't do it then why do we expect our children to do it? How many times have you said 'I have told you before you cannot do that.' Communication is one of the most important things we do in life. We need to communicate at every stage in our lives - to do this we need to listen well.

Children need to learn how to listen, and we as parents need to listen extra carefully because children may not always know the words to express their feelings. Children tend to get angry and are full of emotion and say and do strange things when they are trying to express their feelings, especially if something is wrong in their lives. When problems finally come to light, parents often say, 'if I had only listened to what s/he was trying to say', or 'so that's what s/he was trying to let me know all this time.' A lot of you may already be saying 'yes, maybe I don't take the time to listen enough' or feeling guilty because you just don't have enough time for sitting and having a nice cosy chat. Guilt is a useless emotion, don't waste your feelings on it. Yes, the cosy chat is important, but we must do even more. Every time you are together is an opportunity you have to listen.

So how can we parents become good listeners? And how can we raise our children to be good listeners too? These tips to help you develop good listening habits.

Developing the good listening habit	* First ask yourself a few questions. Who is your child's favourite friend? Do you know what is your child's favourite toy, outing, book, treat, animal, story, film, game? Have you been listening?

* You have some important information to impart. How do you make sure your child listens to you? Ensure you have eye-to-eye contact, even hold the child if you feel more comfortable or so that s/he stays put. Then you can say your piece. Confirm that you are understood: 'Do not go near the hot radiator any more, it is very, very dangerous. Do you understand?' Then wait to get some sort of acknowledgement even if it is just a nod of the head.

* If your child wants to talk to you about something important don't just half listen while you are trying to concentrate on something else. 'Be truthful, say 'I am sorry, I can't listen properly now but when I have finished doing this bit which takes five minutes I'll be all yours.' That honest answer gives your child many lessons in life, having patience being just one of them.

* Practice does make perfect - you get better at evaluating the importance of the message your child wants to get across, after just the first few words. But do take into consideration that a child feels absolutely passionate about most things, and someone breaking a favourite toy may bring forth emotions you wouldn't show if the house fell down.

* Relax while you are listening - it should not be hard work. Once you start thinking 'Oh I am ignoring her, I must try harder to listen', it becomes a chore, forget it. Remind yourself that you are doing something very valuable, you are making your child feel s/he is important to you and helping to build a good self-image.

* The bigger your family gets the more your listening time must be shared. It is a good idea to have a weekly family meeting where each member of the family gets equal time to speak about any problems and to share anything that is going on in the household. Make sure each one has a turn. In our house we pass my daughter's magic wand around the table and the only one allowed to speak is the one holding the magic wand. It works - whoever holds the wand always finds something to say. It may even be something like my daughter said one day 'I am sorry, nothing to say today, I am totally happy with my life' and I thought, Oh how wonderful, I'm certainly glad I heard that.

* If a row is going on, don't make hasty judgements before listening closely to both sides of the story. Ask questions, clarify what is causing the disagreement, and encourage those involved to work out the differences for themselves, to try to come to compromises with your help.

* Ask what would they do in your position. Children can be beautifully honest when they are in the wrong sometimes.

* If you did not listen well and got the wrong end of the stick, apologise and explain why.

* Acknowledge your child's feelings when answering: 'I am sorry you are so upset, but you cannot shout and scream like that, it upsets the whole family, it's not fair.'

* If ever you get angry or have a row with your partner and your child is listening to it, always give an opportunity for her to talk about it with you later. Discuss what made you angry. Let's face it, bottled-up emotions don't do anybody any good. Talk about other ways you could have expressed your anger and other ways in which the behaviour which caused it could be changed. Your child may come up with some great ideas if you listen to her.

* Always respect and acknowledge your child's words even if you do not agree with them.

* Be as honest and open as possible about all things in your home. This encourages an open household where anything can be discussed, including sexual, or unpleasant, hurtful or sad things. This way, your child will be able to confide in you, and will know that anything can be discussed and that you will be fair.

* If at first you keep missing the hidden meaning behind what your child is saying, don't despair. Practice makes perfect, keep trying and you'll end up knowing your child very well.

* Remember it is always quicker to listen carefully than to listen badly, especially in the long run.

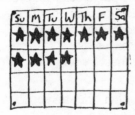

Discipline

In our society discipline tends to be a negative word - it has become associated with punishment. But it shouldn't be something that is imposed on a child. Discipline can be very positive. I exercise regularly, eat a healthy, balanced diet and read regularly and then give a certain amount of my time to people. This is my positive discipline for myself and I enjoy it. It is an inner discipline children need to learn, to discipline themselves for inner rewards, to provide them with a strong sense of control over their own lives. If children learn how to behave simply out of fear, they'll stop being disciplined as soon as they are alone. Effective self-discipline can be learned very early but it can be a slow process.

Children need **guidelines**. Without love and a good example how are our children to become disciplined by us parents? Do aspire to be happy, fulfilled, caring and loving within yourself and this will naturally overflow into your children. Don't be like the old saying 'Do as I say, not as I do'.

Disciplining tips

* Raise your children on **love**.

* Children need **models** more than they need critics or rules and regulations. Be a good model.

* Be **disciplined** yourself.

* Remember how you behaved as a child - the acquisition of self-discipline is a continuous, slow process, sometimes with a small step forward, then many steps back - just keep at it! Remember how we abused our parents at times. Remember too how we resented it if our parents were not perfect, patient and understanding all the time.

* Never **compare** your children with anyone else. Each child is unique!

* Try to teach **self-discipline** in all areas of life, in taking care of health, appearance, homework and in treating others.

* Teach constructive ways of **coping with frustration and anger**. Do role playing on how to deal with specific problems such as teasing and teach how physical activities, like running or punching a pillow can release anger and tension. Teach them to try to calm down and contemplate a problem when they are not so upset. If they pull faces and shout, try putting them in front of a mirror and looking at themselves - they may end up laughing or crying.

* Try not to show negative anger in front of children, remove yourself for a few minutes and direct your anger elsewhere.

* Children may seem to be angry when in fact they are anxious about something - a text or a row with a friend, for example. Be sensitive and **listen**, not challenging or argumentative.

* Make a decision not to participate in family fights, refuse to be part of a war-like atmosphere.

* Give children as much **control** over their lives as possible. Encourage them to make decisions where safety permits. Being told what to do causes frustration levels to rise.

* Always follow through with any punishments you have threatened (if you can). So be sure to make realistic punishments only. If you back down your child will learn you don't mean what you say.

* I find that the most effective punishments are withdrawal of privileges or isolation for a short time.

* Deal with a quick **temper** firmly and quickly, simply stating that it is unacceptable. Remove yourself or them, or even go on strike. You love them, but why should you do things for someone who behaves in such a nasty manner?

* Do not overlook or rationalise an outburst of anger just to avoid a scene. Tantrums are unacceptable behaviour. Teach them to express anger in other ways.

* Do not use fear, hitting or yelling to enforce your code of behaviour or discipline. I know it's hard - we have all lost our cool sometimes but work towards calm as an ideal.

* **Play** with your children regularly.

* **Talk** with your children regularly.

* Avoid telling them off in front of others; no-one likes this, you or them.

* Have a family conference once a week, where each member of the family is allowed to talk and air grievances.

* Use **praise** to get things you want done.

* Kiss, cuddle and tell your children you love them regularly whatever their age. Give them a good self-image and a sense of self-worth.

* Help your child to live life fully.

* Please do not be **negative**. For example, avoid general statements like 'You never help me,' 'you look so scruffy', 'you are inconsiderate.' Instead say 'What would you do if you were me and your child would not help or talked badly to you?', or 'You look great when you take a few minutes to try and you'll feel so much better too.'

* Do not talk at or down to your children. They are not inferior to you because they are yours or younger than you.

* Don't feel you need to be right all the time.

* Do not tease or bait - this will raise the frustration level and lead to arguments.

* Do not give punishments when you are still angry.

* Do not let children watch too much violence on television or video etc, and do talk about it and put it in the correct perspective in real life.

* Do not demand from them more than they are capable of doing. Do not set goals that your child cannot or does not want to achieve. They may not want the life you imagine for them.

* Do not be too materialistic and value things and money more than children, people and love.

* Do not use a hateful angry tone when disciplining your children.

* Don't take your own frustrations in life out on them just because they are smaller.

* I know it's difficult - just do your best, and as my four year old son always pipes up, remember the most important thing is 'loving and caring.'

Breaking nasty
or annoying habits

We often don't know how they began, but suddenly we turn around and become aware of a nasty habit we can't seem to stop them doing. First of all, bear in mind that it is better to ignore annoying behaviour than to make a fuss, because once they know they get attention by doing something upsetting they'll keep doing it. So grit your teeth, ignore the behaviour if possible but if that doesn't work, here are some more suggestions.

What to do about nose-picking

Let's face it, nose-picking is a most annoying habit! If children want to provoke you, nose-picking works.

* A constantly itchy nose could be the symptom of an allergy. Talk to your GP about it, identify and avoid offending foods or substances.

* If they have a cold, teach them to blow their nose well, one nostril at a time and how to clean just inside the nostrils with a paper hanky. Put Vaseline around the nostrils if they get sore.

* Distract children from nose picking, do something constructive like play dough or a jigsaw, or a manual activity.

* Remember nose-picking can be a pleasure (even for adults). Don't deny it altogether, but encourage private explorations!

What to do about spitting

This anti-social habit is usually copied from a little rascal at play-school or they may even copy an 'elderly' rascal. Common especially among boys around four to five years of age.

* Explain immediately that it is unacceptable behaviour and is naughty, messy, dirty etc.

* March them out of the house, or room, saying firmly 'unacceptable'.

* Don't give too much attention to it, just be firm and remove, otherwise they may do it just for the attention. After removal, when they return remind them: 'That sort of behaviour will not be tolerated.'

* If it happens again and again withdraw a treat or pleasure.

What to do about biting	A favourite nasty of the under-fours, biting is like an extension of teething. At first they may not realise the hurt it can cause. From the children's point of view they cannot tell you to leave their toys alone but you'll soon drop toys if your hand is bitten.

* Say 'No' firmly and sharply each time it happens.

* If it happens a lot, try to understand why - is your child trying to tell you something? For example, they may be unhappy at play-school, or they may feel ignored or jealous of a new baby.

* Give extra attention, love and cuddles.

* Let them take a bite at their own hand or arm to show how it hurts or at least feels.

* An old-fashioned remedy was to bite them gently yourself to give them the idea of how it felt, but some psychologists say that brings you down to their level!

* Biting is generally only a phase that passes naturally, but be on your guard to defend others if the phase is at its peak.

Kicking This may be almost an impulsive reflex action to a deeply felt emotion or hurt they haven't learnt yet to control or understand.

* Again say a firm 'No' and remove from the incident - but don't be too dramatic.

* Talk it over, why is your child kicking? If they kick to get a toy back, explain a different or more acceptable way of getting the toy.

* Discuss it, explain that it is unkind to kick or hurt someone. Remind them how they would feel if someone came and kicked them, it's sore, gives a bruise or cut or red lump and so on. The description you give obviously depends on the age of your child.

* If repeated, withdraw privileges and insist on an apology being given.

What to do about lying All children are capable of lying as soon as they start talking, usually it's harmless, it's part of experimenting with talking and it's interesting to see what happens. But if it happens constantly:

* Let your child know and understand it is unacceptable behaviour, then distract attention by doing something entirely different.

* Lying is often a cry for attention. It sometimes occurs if there has been an emotional trauma at home. Extra attention may be all that is needed.

* Try a light approach - if your child has a dirty face but tells you it's washed, answer: 'Well, funny, I could have sworn I saw a dirty face just pass me by' - a half-joke may soften the reprimand.

* Or just say 'Let's try that one again - action replay.' Eventually the truth may out.

* Try talking about the idea of right and wrong.

* Just answer back quickly 'Of course you haven't - go and do it now - there's a love.'

* If your child is lying about possessions, try to work out the logic by discussion. 'Why did you say that Dad had a Mercedes? Is it because you want one?' Maybe it is just a way of bringing fairytales to *real life*. But the distinction between fiction and fantasy should be made clear by parents so as not to hurt anyone.

Thumb-sucking

Thumb-sucking fills a need for security, so it's not always a bad habit. However, excessive thumb-sucking can change the shape of a child's mouth and put teeth out of alignment permanently.

* Don't over-react initially, it may disappear.

* Give an orthodontic soother instead when at the baby stage.

* Paint on the 'nasty' substances you can get in the chemist especially for the purpose.

* Make or buy a finger puppet for that special finger, give it a name, say it does not like to be sucked.

* Put a kiss or imaginary treasure into each hand at bedtime and tell your child to hold on tight so as not to lose them.

* Have thumb-sucking rules. For example, thumb-sucking only allowed in the bedroom. This limits the behaviour and makes it a lonely, undesirable act.

* It may sound like blackmailing but you could pay her a small amount daily or weekly as a reward for not thumb-sucking. This really works on the older children and it gives them great motivation.

* Ask the dentist to explain how thumb-sucking may damage teeth.

Soothers
Dummies, Do Do's, whatever your name for them, once the habit is started, it can be difficult to break. Here are a few suggestions.

* Put a bitter tasting solution on it, for example vinegar, so that your child won't enjoy the taste. This works in some cases, but I'm not too keen on this idea.

* Whatever method you choose to remove the soother, give plenty of warning before the hour or day the soother goes, so they are prepared for the parting.

* Then just get rid of it and be consistent, no replacement given. Otherwise it will be harder next time.

* Gradually limit use of the soother. Put it under the pillow

IT WAS HER NOT ME

all day and keep it safe for night times only. Then a little suck before bed and under the pillow it goes.

* Finally give it to the soother fairy who takes them back to soother-land.

* Start a little hole in the dummy so the shape is not so appealing.

* Always try to coordinate the loss of the soother with a replacement comfort toy. For example, the fairy may have left a tiny teddy in its place under the pillow.

Masturbation * Playing with private parts is normal and natural for both sexes. Ignore it and distract attention.

* Don't scold or make the child feel guilty.

* As they get older, explain it's their special private part of their body that makes babies and touching it is a private thing to be done when alone.

* The social unacceptability of the habit will become apparent as they mix with others and the habit will lessen, at least in company.

Temper tantrums A child's tantrum is always a cry for help. It is a clear loud message 'I can't cope', 'I can't deal with all that is going on inside me.' That's easy to understand but usually these temper tantrums come at a time when we parents are also under stress. So even the most patient of parents can be forgiven for seeing red when their child has yet another temper tantrum.

* Tantrums tend to peak at approximately two years old. Then gradually they ease off until the age of five, when only about 10% of children are still having temper tantrums. In young children tantrums frequently occur because the child has difficulty in communicating and because they are starting to become aware of their own individuality and identity. So they start asserting themselves and their needs.

* Would you believe that around two years old, two or three tantrums a day, lasting five to ten minutes is thought to be normal? This temper stage does pass naturally, but a child has to learn how to live with other people and be considerate of their needs. We need to set limits, it's not easy. They need careful parenting to help them control and change their behaviour. Parents too need extra help and support at this stage. Make sure you get plenty of rest and time away from this lovable but temperamental little darling.

Tactics to deal with tantrums

* What's the message your child is giving you? It helps to try to understand what caused the anger in the first place, then you can prevent it from happening again.

* A common reason for tantrums is being overtired. Keep to the sleep and rest routine as much as possible. The tired child can just go crazy.

* A sickly child tends to be very irritable, try to compensate by being indulgent, and letting them have their own way a bit more when they're unwell to avoid distress.

* Dressing time can be stressful and tempers can flare - try not to do battle, it's not worth it. A regular routine helps. Try dressing while still in the cot when they can't wait to get up. They may be more co-operative.

* Toilet training can get annoying for the child and the parents. Take it slow and easy, don't expect too much. Start late, stay calm.

* Allergic reaction to certain foods may cause hyperactivity or may be linked with excessive tantrums. Watch out for this if there are allergies in the family. Keep away from foods containing lots of additives, preservatives and colourants.

* Meal times can become another battle ground. If they realise that by refusing food they upset you - they'll do it again! So try not to make a fuss about food. Serve it, and hope for the best; if it's not eaten, take it away and serve it again.

* A very hungry child is more likely to be unreasonable, so don't let them get over-hungry.

* Watch out for danger times. A common time for a tantrum is after an exciting event, or following nursery school, or when they have been away from you. It's a good idea to give lots of attention at these times.

* Do not be blackmailed. Remember that the more often your children get their own way after a tantrum - the more they'll do it. Stand firm. Don't give in.

* Distract them before they reach boiling point. For example, ask them to help you, talk about a future outing, even look at the big truck outside, produce a toy, anything!

* Give a warning. 'If you don't stop that, you'll get very upset,' or 'I'll leave the room' or 'To act like that you must be tired, I'll put you to bed' or 'You'll have no time to finish your game' or make it a joke. 'Let me get a mirror

pand show you that face you're pulling. It will frighten everybody', or 'Gosh, poor floor, stamping it like that will make a hole', or 'The dog's run away. He thinks you've turned into a monster'. Take your pick!

If a child gets totally out of control

* Hold the child tight, facing away from you, arms down. Whilst holding, whisper things to try to calm them down.

* Isolate the child, remove to a separate room, or facing the corner, or back to the cot for a length of time, to calm both you and the child.

* Activity **time out** - meaning the out-of-control child is not allowed to join in the game, only watch.

Afterwards

* Teach other ways of expressing anger by doing some form of exercise or saying in words what is causing the anger inside. Also show by example. Don't you lose your temper. Explain why you are angry and be prepared to apologise. Expect them to do the same. Chart any progress.

* Have a rewards or star chart, so that the focus is moved from bad behaviour to good behaviour. Reward good behaviour, ignore bad as much as possible.

* Always give your children enough attention and listen to them. Let them know you love them all the time.

* Vomiting or breath-holding at the beginning or end of a tantrum is not unusual. These are very difficult for parents to cope with but the best way of dealing with them is to play them down - just clear up the vomit without comment. The breath-holding is worrying but after a few seconds they will start breathing again; the less fuss made the better.

* If tantrums continuously occur after the age of five or if you feel your child may have a behaviourial problem, do go and chat with your GP. It could have a physical or psychological origin.

* Be observant. Children who have communication difficulties may have more tantrums. Excessive tantrums can occasionally be a sign of deafness, language difficulties or slow development. If you suspect this check it out with your GP.

* It always helps to talk to other parents who are going through the same thing. At least you can be reassured you are not the only parent who felt like joining in and having a tantrum too.

Jealousy

In each and every family where there is more than one child the green eyed monster jealousy often raises its head. The questions parents usually ask are all very similar. 'How can we prepare our child for the arrival of a new sister or brother?'. 'What can we do to prevent or at least limit the amount of jealousy she feels?'. 'What do we do if he shows obvious signs of jealousy, or even gets violent with his new brother or sister?' The age of your first child will influence how s/he acts towards the new arrival, but the reaction also depends on how parents handle the situation. Children may feel left out, unloved, and jealous, it's only natural. But sometimes parents can exacerbate a child's jealousy. Mothers getting pregnant for the second time may feel guilty that they are in a way deserting their first child, or may feel they will deprive the first child in some way, and feel they may not have enough love to share around. They fear diluting the intense love they feel for their first born. Well, it is not true and speaking as child number three, I always felt loved, not just by my parents but by my sisters as well, so the parents are helped out by loving from the whole family. It even sometimes helps to level out a parent-child relationship and helps the child become more independent.

And that is what being a parent is all about - parents can guide but then must step aside. A parent is there not just to pick children up after a fall but also to teach them how to get up by themselves. Do remember that however careful, thoughtful, and loving you are, some jealousy is bound to happen, so when they say things like 'you can take the baby back now, I don't like it any more' or give darling sister a hug that nearly makes her blue, or even if your usually wonderful child gives her sister a blow that would put a professional boxer to shame, don't be surprised. It happens to the best of children and families at times. With lots of love and support from caring parents this little green eyed monster will turn back to your little darling once more.

Ways of preventing and coping with jealousy

* **Prepare** your child well for the new arrival. Let them share in your pregnancy and appreciate the growing baby inside.

* Some parents like to wait until the bump is obvious, before telling children about the new baby on the way. I find that children forget the baby's inside the womb for long stretches so there is no harm in telling them early.

* Once you are nearing the end of pregnancy encourage them to feel the baby kicking and to talk to the baby. Listen to music together: your child, the baby (inside mum), mum and dad.

* Show your children **photos**, if you have them, of you

when you where pregnant with them inside your tummy.
Then go through the pictures of when they were just born
and gradually go through their development so they will
understand what is going on. Talk about them as well as
the new baby.

* Try to pick out photographs of them dirty, or crying, or
  being bold - these will come in handy later to say, 'yes,
  you cried a lot too, look at the pictures'.

* Once they have a good grasp of all that is going to
  happen you may be surprised at how remarkably well
  they adapt.

* Explain all that is in store, that you will have to go into
  hospital for a few days, that they can come and visit and
  see their new sister or brother and then you'll come home
  with the baby.

* Try to keep your family routine going along smoothly
  even though you may be waiting to go into labour or in
  hospital. Continuing with routine life will give a feeling
  of security.

* Encourage as much **independence** as possible before the
  baby is born, it is good for your children and will help
  you out too. There may be many times when you will be
  busy with the baby later on.

* The idea of all the children exchanging little **gifts** is one
  that worked well in my family. I picked the gifts with
  care, just small things, but what I knew they would love.
  They were very impressed with their new baby. Of
  course the obvious questions may be asked 'how did she
  get that from out of your tummy?' or 'did you buy this,
  come on?' so be prepared, but they generally love any
  excuse to get a present anyway.

* **Fathers** are of tremendous value at this time. Make sure
  you do plenty of the childcare routines, like bathing -
  even start a new fun hobby you can all do together.

* Once the baby is born encourage the other children to
  help you care for the new baby.

* Put a stool near to the changing area so they can watch
  the changing routines.

* Encourage them to be mother and baby's helper, let them
  hold, sing and talk to the baby. Do show your
  appreciation for all help. But don't overdo the 'little
  helper' bit as they can get fed up with it too.

* Keep to the same meal times, bedtime story and so on.

Give the older child that extra special attention just before bed, story, cuddles, a time that you can share together away from the baby if possible.

* **Bath time** together is always a pleasant way to form family bonds.

* Catch **visitors** and ensure they show the older child attention first before they fuss over the baby, then the older child can join in showing the new baby off.

* It is nice if visitors do bring a treat, however small, for the other children in the family. But in case they don't, have a few little treats put by so you can bring them out quickly if the need arises.

* Do let your upset show in moderation if you are tired of the baby's crying or whatever, and let the children do the same. Let them see the love and joy baby brings too, but allowing them to see a balanced emotional response means they will not be afraid to show any negative feelings they may have about the baby too.

* Give the older child special new privileges, like staying up later, or pocket money increase.

* Let them know that they are the **baby's teacher.** They can teach how to smile, laugh, talk, love, and lots more - if they show, the baby will learn and copy.

* **Grandparents** too are of great help at this time. It is great if they give plenty of love and attention to the other children to help them deal with the separation and develop new love attachments

* It is generally not a good idea to be **over-protective** of the older children or over-anxious about the effect the new arrival has on them. Over-anxious attention is more harmful than good and doesn't give them a chance to find other love bonds and attachments or independence.

* When you first arrive from the hospital let someone else carry the baby when the older child first sees you. Play up the excitement of being home and seeing them again, and play down the excitement of bringing home the new baby.

* Most children misbehave, wanting to gain attention. For example, crying for something just as you start to feed the baby, or breaking things, regressing in habits, like wetting pants again, or wanting a bottle again just to be like the baby and whining to get more attention - this is natural.

* Because all children tend to get **jealous** one way or another, it is a wise precaution not to leave the baby unattended with your other child, especially if the other child is under five and showing any tendency to be jealous.

* If your child ever hits the baby, stay calm but be absolutely firm, remove from the incident, get eye to eye contact, holding firmly and explain that it is not acceptable behaviour. You could put it like this: 'when you were a little baby we treasured you and would not let anything or anyone harm you. We all must protect and look after the baby now, no hitting, I know the crying may upset you sometimes, it does me too, but hitting is never acceptable, let's go and say we are sorry now.' I firmly believe in saying you're sorry too, if not in the heat of the moment then later.

* Letting the older child go to **play school** or something similar can help cure jealousy but do it cleverly, do not make it look as if you are getting rid of them. Start the play school before baby arrives or at a convenient time when some time has lapsed.

* If signs of jealousy show keep the child as busy and occupied as possible so the jealousy is not allowed to fester.

* It may be an idea, if possible, to have a special place for older children to go and play where the baby cannot disturb them.

* Be prepared for them to show feelings of jealousy at some stage, if not at the beginning then a couple of months later when all the excitement is over.

* The only cure for jealousy is to give the older children as much of your time, attention and love as you can. Doing all you can to make them feel that they are still very important to you. It is a mistake though to become over-protective. The best way to avoid naughty, attention-seeking behaviour is to ignore it as much as possible; if it doesn't work they will stop it. And do try to appreciate and applaud any attempts they may make to overcome jealousy.

* Keep **loving**, and jealousy passes.

* Children (and adults) tend only to be jealous when they feel **insecure**. Give your children a good self-image and family security and they should not feel the need to be jealous of anyone.

Handling arguments

Do your children's squabbles get you down? Do you sometimes think that you would dearly love to have a peaceful household? Do you despair telling them to share and be nice to each other? Console yourself that the same arguments between sisters and brothers are going on pretty well everywhere. Although it may upset you to hear them rowing, do remember that through these conflicts they are learning and developing their own sense of identity. All children tend to have slight 'Jekyll and Hyde' personalities. They feel passionate and strong about everything. Children do need our guidance but we are often tempted to still the water at the first sign of trouble. Instead, children must learn how to cope with difficulties themselves without resorting to screaming or violence. So how and when to break up the screaming match is very important.

To encourage social skills such as sharing, encourage mixing with other children from the earliest age. But do not expect too much from the very young. Try to have an open household where all friends are welcome even if it does mean a lot of extra work for you. Encourage generosity and praise any generous gestures and acts. Even if you don't want a lick of that horrible looking ice lolly - take it, at least they're trying, so give praise for the effort. Make sure your children feel secure and loved, that they see sharing going on, and they'll follow the example you set. Do not go around constantly saying 'stop that fighting, you are always rowing.' Make a list of simple rules that you think are most important to keep and stick to them. Be consistent and firm. Don't allow children to manipulate you, whatever their age. If you let them get their own way too often you are doing them and yourself a disservice. Children are just not capable of being in a position to know what is best for them. So parents who fare well in the family peace-stakes are the ones who are firm and give the children firm, secure limits they know they cannot cross.

Tips to stop squabbling	
*	Firstly identify with the child's **feeling**, saying something like 'you sound very angry and upset. What's happening?'
*	Try to find out what exactly is the **cause** of the row.
*	Let the children know you **understand** fully - listen carefully to each one's point of view.
*	Explain the problem back to them and tell them they are very good, intelligent children and now that they have had time to think about it you are sure they can **work it out** together. Then leave the room - it's worth a try.
*	It's worth asking whether fighting is for real or not, as some children can enjoy playing rough sometimes. But do tell them the rule is that the play-fighting stops if one

of them stops liking it.

* If the fighting is for real, stay **calm**, separate them and explain how awful it is to watch them hurting each other. Later, calmly discuss why and how the fight came about and ways it could be prevented in the future.

* If children are sharing a room, or anything, have a well-defined area which belongs to each of them and have share-plans organised.

* Arguments can often happen if children have to spend too much time in a confined space at close quarters. Get them **outdoors** whenever possible with plenty of space and company to defuse any explosive energy.

* Avoid making snap decisions and **judgements** about who was to blame, and doling out punishments. You could misunderstand the situation and get it wrong, which looks very unjust.

* Show your children how to **compromise**. Suggest, for example, that if they both want to ride the tractor, one can sit in the trailer until the end of the garden, then swap around. Give alternatives they can relate to without them having to back down.

* **Never take sides**.

* Try not to get angry yourself, but keep calm and remember that once children reach the age of seven or so, they generally become more **self-controlled**.

* If older children are still losing control and rowing or fighting a lot, look carefully at the example you as parents are setting, or look for an underlying cause.

* Never talk down to children, or treat them as inferior beings just because they are smaller and younger than you are. No one likes to be talked down to.

* Don't reprimand them in front of others, it's a terrible blow to anyone's pride. Take them aside if you have something to say.

* There is no such thing as a bad child, it is always wise to emphasise this. It is the **behaviour** that is bold or unacceptable, not the child. The child is always good and loved.

* If ever you do need to **punish** a child for something, always be certain they know the reason why. For example, 'you simply cannot throw a fit of temper and hit your brother like that. You hurt your brother and ruin everyone's right to have a peaceful and happy home. Go

to your room and stay there until you can control yourself and be kinder to us all.'

* Angry outbursts often recur in children because they work. When anger goes unchecked in children it can become a family-manipulator. Teach children the silliness of trying to use anger as a means of getting their own way. Teach them to express anger in constructive ways and teach them to use their minds. Learning to use our minds **creatively** avoids the pain of anger.

* Teach them to exercise **discipline** on themselves so that fighting becomes unnecessary (see tips on **Discipline**).

What to expect

* *Under one year old* Your baby seems to be a bundle of wants and needs. They just do not understand right and wrong. You do not have to shout or hit, by the tone of your voice they will know you disapprove. They love you and will want to do everything to please you - praise good behaviour. A firm voice is the best way to handle the situation.

* *Age one to two* They will be exploring and into all sorts of mischief. Instead of saying 'No' all the time make your house childproof and clear the way for roaming hands. Then let them develop naturally, saying 'No' only when really necessary.

* *Age three to four* Don't tell them what to do all the time or they will try to do the opposite. This is the age of self-assertion, of your child saying 'no', 'I won't', and throwing tantrums. Use good psychology, instead of just saying 'stop it', distract: if you want them to do something make it fun, a race, a game to share, 'stop fighting, you two; let's play!'

* *Age five to seven* I love this age - they are so willing to please. OK, they may have their arguments but you can reason with them. Give them time to think about it and they'll come round. Praise works wonders. They may often start to be cute and not hear what you have said, feigning deafness, or daftness more like it. Give plenty of warnings and time to think about things and you'll get by happily.

* *Age eight to ten* At this age they will want to be treated a bit more as an adult, with explanations and polite requests, rather than commands of 'stop that' and 'no, you cannot.' To get them to do as you say may take a lot of reminding, discussions on conduct and so on, but it will be worth the time and effort to avoid conflicts and fights.

Television

Whether you like television or not, once you have one in your home it can become part of everyday life. Figures researchers have come up with in the USA are frightening - one report stated that the average child watches three to five hours of television daily. But the television need not be the parents' enemy and the children's friend, if you use it well and wisely. The television can be controlled and used as a positive learning experience for the entire family.

Once you decide that you want to have a television you must then decide what programmes your children can watch and how much television time they are allowed. You could even write down a viewing schedule so everyone knows what they can do and view. One child psychologist suggested two hours viewing as maximum for young children. Be flexible from day to day but remember that watching television is time away from real life learning and experiences. Young children must also learn by doing and playing as well as watching.

With these points in mind here are some tips that may make television viewing a positive instead of a negative experience for all of the family. Use the television as an opportunity to get family co-operation. Resolving conflicts of who watches what and when can be a good opportunity to use diplomacy and achieve family fair play.

Tips on TV viewing

* Remember that once the television is on your children are exposed to whatever is showing. Even if they seem to be playing with toys they may absorb much more than you realise, so be careful what you have on when the children are around.

* For all young children avoid frightening, scary or overwhelming broadcasts. The world is a dangerous, frightening place. There is no need for your child to see horrific war zones at the tender age of three, they may decide the world is an evil place, and could start all sorts of imaginings and nightmares.

* Programmes for the pre-school child should be short, educational and full of action, singing and rhymes.

* Programmes should show a clear distinction between fantasy and reality, otherwise the child may get confused as to what is real and what is not. Talk about this and teach them to be clear about fantasy and reality. Explain what actors are, and how cartoons are made from pictures.

* In general show programmes that stimulate play. Programmes emphasising sharing and consideration for others, for example, *Bosco*, *Play School*, *Play Bus*, and *Sesame Street*.

* Watching TV with your children is a good idea, then you can follow the programme up with conversation about the subject it covered and something creative, for example, drawing a picture, making a puppet, visiting the zoo where the animals can be seen in real life.

* Cartoons like *Postman Pat*, *Fireman Sam*, *Thomas The Tank Engine*, can give an opportunity for children to see another way of life.

* Some fairy tales are a delight to watch but others can be frightening - always watch your children's reaction and don't be afraid to turn it off and give an explanation. 'There is too much fighting and hitting in that story. You know there are much better ways of settling differences than fighting each other.'

* Do participate when the opportunity arises - dancing, singing and making up rhymes together, enjoy yourself too.

* Remember TV is a passive pastime - children need action, movement and play too.

* Once you set limits, stick to them, and be consistent. If need be, set a timer or an alarm clock and once viewing time is over - turn the box off.

* Make sure you plan alternatives, don't just leave them sitting there looking at an empty screen, or they will get discontented. Children often watch television because they are bored, so plan other activities.

* When trying to cut down on viewing time discuss with your children alternative things they may like to do. Ask for their suggestions, get them involved.

* Only have the television on when someone is actively watching it.

* Avoid using the TV as a babysitter but do take a well earned rest and view it with your children, or peel the potatoes whilst the cartoons are on, sitting next to them.

* Have a discussion about advertising and commercials, during the children's programme times - they tend to be bombarded with commercials for expensive toys. Help your children to become consumer-wise. Explain what advertisements are, that they try to make you buy the product so they can make money. Explain about the special effects making toys look larger and more appealing. The older child could even do a survey on the commercials shown at different times and how they differ and change depending on who is watching.

* Let TV enrich your child's imagination by acting out the stories they watch maybe using different endings.

* If some special event is on like Wimbledon or the World Cup, make the watching of this a big family event - have a picnic whilst watching the tennis, do coaching of tennis or football after the show. Start your own sports league, make a scrap-book following the whole event or series.

* If you have a video recorder then record the television programmes you want and watch them at a time that is more convenient for you.

* Encourage your children to get involved, join any clubs, write to the presenters of programmes, save bits and bobs for making things on the craft programmes.

* If you are seriously worried about your children becoming TV addicts, try to get them interested in a new activity or hobby and gradually reduce their box-watching time.

* Have one day a week where no television is allowed and plan ahead what you can all do instead.

* During weekly family discussion time, decide the viewing for the week with the TV programmes guide. Keep meal times, bedtimes and homework times in mind - then stick to it.

* Examine your own viewing of the television regularly - are you setting a good example? Be careful of what you watch too. If you just vegetate in front of the box every evening, then your children will copy your example. And in my view you miss out on life if you watch too much of the square box.

Getting out
and about
with children

The secret of successful travelling with children is to plan the journey well. What you will need depends on how you travel, how long it takes and where you end up. So sit down with your partner and plan a long journey. Or be at the ready with your **out bag** prepared for any little adventurous outing. Remember many hands make light work, so take a pal! But don't be too ambitious if you've just had a baby - exhaustion sets in very quickly. Be well rested before the journey and make it a great adventure. Describing things, finding out about different places, even the most mundane bus trip can be exciting - go upstairs to get a good view. Guess the stops and who is getting on and off. Being a bit thoughtful in advance will pay dividends. Before children (BC) we could just up and off, now we have to think twice and we may feel we take everything with us but the kitchen sink. Do encourage the children who are old enough to take their own back-pack or holder to carry their own food, games and other needs. It encourages taking responsibility, independence, sharing and kindness.

Trains, boats, cars and kids

* An **out bag** is a good idea. Have this packed at the ready in your car or in the cupboard by the front door. Have bag, will travel!

The **out bag** should contain: disposable nappies, a moist flannel in a plastic bag or moist wipes, a plastic bag for dirty nappy, a terry nappy or something to lean on and dry with, toys or books if distraction is needed, vaseline or bottom cream (if wanted) and paper tissues.

For a long trip, add: baby food, instant dry-type better for travelling; beaker, bottle containing milk or juice. Change of clothes. Older children might like mini juice cartons and snacks, biscuits etc. Avoid salty snacks or they'll get too thirsty. Yes, you've got it! More drinks and more toilet stops!

* Ensure you and the children travel in comfort. For baby use a sling or back-pack or buggy. Don't tire toddlers out walking too far.

* When travelling dress the children in layers (like an onion) so you can peel off dirty layers or slip one off if it becomes too hot.

Cars * Take extra pillows and blankets if it's a long journey.

* Hang a cloth shoe-holder over a front seat and put in games (magnetic ones are good), books, toys, cassettes (with favourite music) to keep them occupied.

* Evening or night is the best time to travel long distance so little ones sleep.

* Plan plenty of car games such as 'I Spy' or 'Find the car numbers' when boredom creeps in. Tell stories, sing songs - it can be great fun.

* Have a rubbish bag in the car so it doesn't get too messy. And an extra bag in case of travel sickness.

* Don't give rich or heavy food for a couple of hours prior to the journey.

* Keep an extra toy supply in the boot.

* Get an anti-static trailer attached to the car.

* Have frequent stops for fresh air and stretching legs during day time travelling.

* If a child is usually sick, get a travel or sea band from the chemist or teach how to apply pressure with thumb to the middle of the wrist to stop sickness. Try making a home-made band with a watch strap and a button.

* If travelling long distance at night give travel sickness medicine.

* Always think of safety first - restrain all children properly in seats or cots, remove all loose objects from the back window.

Trains * Trains are exciting and don't usually cause sickness and there's more space, but don't rely on buffet cars. Take your own refreshments.

* Add games to the **out bag** - you can also read more easily on the train, so story books and quiz or activity books are handy to have with you.

Boats * If taking a long journey by boat, get a cabin, it is worth the extra money.

* Give all the family sea or travel bands and hope for a smooth crossing.

* Again put plenty of activity games in the **out bag**.

* Do make it an adventure - look around the boat - talk to the sailors, encourage them to take an interest in everything going on, on the boat.

* Spend a lot of time in the fresh air on deck, but if you feel sick, lie down.

Air travel * Let's face it - it is the quickest way to travel with young children, and quicker travelling is a great advantage.

* Get there early to avoid queues.

* Go aboard all freshened up, with clean nappies etc.

* When you make reservations, state that children will be travelling and if a baby or toddlers are with you ask for bulkhead seats with extra space. Also specify window seats if wanted.

* Take a sling for baby to keep your hands free.

* Add to **out bag**: Sweets (for sucking as the plane lands and takes off); extra drinks (avoid fizzy ones); bouncing seat if used; extra clothes.

* Don't try to eat a lot of food and drink when holding baby.

* Ask the cabin crew for any help you need.

* Ensure all the family have passports and any special inoculations that may be needed at your destination.

* If any member of the family is on a special diet, for example, food allergies, vegetarian order it when booking and mention it as you check in.

Extra tips * Personal stereos with a variety of favourite tapes are great for the older child.

* When packing nappies add one extra for each hour travelling, just in case.

* Do involve all of your children in the planning of the holiday or outing. The more they understand, the more enjoyment they'll get from the experience.

Getting ready for school

Can you remember the days of the old school yard? It may seem like yesterday or a million light years away to some parents. Whatever your school days where like, try to make school a very positive experience for your children. From the very first mention of the word, talk about it in enjoyable terms. Most parents these days like to send their children to some sort of pre-school play group to ready them for school. It does have the advantage of giving the child a chance to socialise with other children and gain a bit of independence before proper school starts. In surveys, the children who had been to some form of play school found the transition to big school less traumatic than those who had not. But it is a very personal decision and depends on each family's set of circumstances. Some parents may feel that with a little effort they can provide all the learning and social experiences at home that their child may need, or some parents may feel that emotionally they or their children are just not ready for the separation yet. I always feel that parents know best but do make sure you are thinking of what is best for your child, not you. Sometimes it is hard to let go of our little beloved.

There is an abundance of nurseries, creches, kindergartens, and Montessori schools, so look for the one that suits your child's character best.

Before school
* Play **pretend school** at home to prepare for the experience when it comes. Get other children to play the game with you - older children could be helpful here.

* Buy a book on starting school and read it together.

* Talk about your own **first day at school** and how you were very excited but a bit apprehensive too. Explain how you got on and made new friends, it felt strange at first but you got to love going in and looked forward to it. Don't say school is fantastic, just be realistic, warm and optimistic.

* Make sure they can understand simple **instructions** before starting school and tell them what the teacher may say and do.

* Ensure they know how to **dress themselves** and how to **go to the toilet alone**.

* Select new **school clothes** together - make them easy to get on and off and easily washable, try to make it fun.

* Attach **name tags** to all clothes and bags, especially coats, cardigans and shoes.

* Get your child into a **routine** habit of selecting clothes for the morning before going to bed, laying them out, and getting dressed before breakfast.

* Buy a small **school bag** - the light weight back-packs are good.

* Buy your children's **school books** early, before August, and avoid the school rush.

* Ask at the school if they operate a second-hand book system.

* If you have older children, check that you do not have the used books lying around at home somewhere.

* Cover all of your children's school books - they last longer that way. Use old wallpaper, or keep wrapping paper that is not too damaged from Christmas and birthdays.

* Visit the school and teacher before the new term starts. Some schools have a visiting day that gives everyone an opportunity to meet. Go to this, walk around the classroom and school - ensure your children understand the lay-out so they won't feel too lost. Find out where the toilet is (very important), the classroom, play area, the cloakroom, and where the head teacher is too.

* Go to the school at different times during the summer, using the route you will use when school starts so it will be familiar.

* Go to the bus stop, or where the school bus will stop. Discuss what it will be like on the first day - you also could mention **road safety** at the same time.

* Make sure they understand who can collect them from school, and explain that they must never go home with anyone else.

* Make sure they know their **name, address** and **telephone number**.

* It will be an advantage to already know how to **count** to ten and say the **alphabet** and be familiar with the practice of looking at story books with you. Don't forget you are the child's natural teacher.

* Set up a night time and morning routine before school starts so you can get into a good habit and continue it naturally as school commences.

* Give your child a special gift to **celebrate** starting school, it could be a new school bag, or a funny-faced alarm clock or whatever is appropriate to your child.

* If a **comfort toy** is special to your child, it could be taken to school at first, it will promote a feeling of security during the day.

* The first school day can be very daunting for the child but it can be emotionally traumatic for the parent too - if you are upset, which is only natural, try not to let it show.

School days * If your child screams and wants to leave with you, gently reassure, talk to the teacher, explain that you are coming back at lunch time. The teacher may let you stay a while longer but when the final moment comes, be strong, let them know when you'll be back and go. Stay around outside to reassure yourself that all is OK, but don't let them see you and they should settle down after a while. I know myself how hard this is to do, but you must give your child the chance to settle in without you. Have a little cry at home, a lot of parents do, crying is a natural emotion that does us all good sometimes.

* Always make sure you are **on time** picking them up from school during the early school days, or they may feel very frightened that you will never come or have left them for good.

* **Be prepared** - school will not bring an immediate improvement in intelligence, manners or behaviour so don't expect too much. In fact some children behave very boldly at home at first because of the whole change and school can be very tiring for little ones. So if they become more clinging, bold, shy or withdrawn, wait a while - it may be just a temporary reaction.

* At the end of each school day, ask about what happened at school. And listen carefully, so you will be able to understand and spot any trouble brewing quickly.

* Make sure at first you give extra time to sit and cuddle and talk when they first come home. If they are exhausted and behave badly try to be understanding and give them extra loving care. The bad behaviour will not last.

* If as time goes on your child is really unhappy at school, go in and discuss things with the teacher. Together, work out if there is anything either of you can do to help, for example changing the seating arrangements, encouraging friendships. Try to judge if this is just a passing phase.

97

* Try to encourage any **friendships**, let them start school with a friend, or bring any budding friend home after school to play.

* Any symptoms like nightmares or bedwetting should be discussed and acted upon straight away, giving reassurance and understanding, never scolding. This is a difficult time for them (see tips on **Bedwetting** and **Sleeping problems**).

* Share and talk about the new routine. Find out all about the teacher, friends, routine, lessons, emotions. Get to understand how they feel and are coping with the new surroundings

* In short, the best thing you can give during the first weeks of school is plenty of your time and attention and of course lots of loving tender care.

Other ideas *   Stick **messages to teacher** on to the coat of a young child with a nappy pin or use a sticky label.

* If problems persist and you have started your child at school very young before four and a half years old, don't be afraid to discuss pulling them out and trying again next year when they are older and emotionally more able to cope.

* If you ever feel that there is a problem with a particular teacher or school discuss the matter with the head. If the problem does not resolve itself and you think a school change would be good, be brave and do it.

* Have a **timer** you can set either for dressing for school or for play-time prior to school, it prepares the child for accepting timetables. It's good for accepting bedtime too.

* Encourage talk about school but don't badger with questions all the time.

* Do try to remember teachers' names, the subjects your children take, and school friends' names. If they keep having to tell you them they'll think you are not listening or are just not interested.

* As the **older child** changes to a new school, stick to the same ideas but remember that your child may be going through many changes inside at this time too, as puberty changes often occur at the same time as secondary school changes. Again give plenty of time, attention and love.

Developing your child's intelligence

Parents are their children's first teachers - even when the children are at school. Do not underestimate your role in your child's intellectual development. Some parents may be wary of confusing the child or may not know how to start encouraging their child to be an independent thinker. But from the day your child is born you can encourage a free thinker with a good self- image, confident to try out new adventures.

Children develop half of their total adult intellectual capacity by the time they are four years old. So it is important to start early. By providing your children with a stimulating environment, you help their talents to develop. The atmosphere and the relationship you have with your child in your home is also important. Don't let them be labelled as 'not bright' or 'naughty' or any of those very damaging labels. Let the children know you have confidence in their abilities. Teach them to understand that mistakes are natural and are something we learn from. All children are born full of curiosity and it is our responsibility not to stifle that curiosity by confining the baby to a play-pen all day or by making them too frightened to explore their own house in case they do some damage. This urge to explore should be actively encouraged at every age. We as parents can preserve, enhance and channel that bubbling spring of our child's wonderful mind. Encouraging their active involvement is the key, so here are some ways in which we can cultivate a child's mind.

Raising an intelligent child

* **Talk, describe, sing** and **play** with your child from birth. Describe what you are doing, what you are eating, where you are. Talk in complete sentences, point out the names for objects around your home.

* **Read out aloud** to them from birth, let them look at the pictures in the books.

* Have plenty of things around for them to look at, touch and explore.

* Ensure your child's **diet** is nutritious. Give a good breakfast, with as little refined carbohydrates as possible. Cut out tea and coffee and fizzy drinks. Small children generally prefer frequent small meals to three large ones. Make sure they get plenty of vitamins and minerals to keep that brain ticking over. Give vitamin supplements if necessary.

* Encourage them to ask **questions**: 'If the weather is dry what will we do?' 'who does the dry weather affect apart from us?' 'How will it affect the garden, the country, the animals, the farmer, the world?' Encourage them to look outside their own little world.

* Encourage **pretend games** - let them pretend or imagine they are objects or animals. Get them to describe how it feels to have a tail, fly in the sky, or whatever.

* Put on little **plays** and **role-play** regularly. Let your child play the heroine, the beggar, the old person, let them act it out and describe how it feels. It teaches them to see the world from a different point of view.

* Get them to imagine a picture to go with a word or a story. Let them **illustrate** any story they hear or write, or do a drawing of an outing or special occasion afterwards.

* Encourage them to think back and **remember** by asking about things that happened in the past, get them to **plan ahead**, to tomorrow or next week.

* Cut out pictures from magazines and newspapers and keep them in a folder. Use these for all sorts of projects, for example a **scrap-book** on the World Cup, the Wimbledon tennis tournament, the general election, a fashion scrap-book, the list is endless.

* Actively encourage any **hobbies** or outside interests - they may even become a future career!

* Writing a **diary** is a great way for children to improve their communication and memory skills.

* Encourage the love of **books**, remembering that children learn from example and use your local **library** to the full.

* Develop their skill of **observation**, play games that make them look closely and memorise things. Ask what clothes someone was wearing, or look at facial expressions, asking 'is she happy, or sad? What makes you think that?'

* Have **painting** or drawing competitions, give marks for overall merit, and the good use of colour, form, perspective, originality, warmth, humour, movement. Make them think about what they are doing and why. Let the children join in and participate in the marking.

* Play **thought-provoking games**, for example what images do the colour green cause in your mind? Grass, gardens, sickness, envy, why? Use a dictionary to help.

* Think of a word, object or person and say the words that they associate with it and why?

* Expand the games they usually play like *snap* or *snakes and ladders*, bringing in new rules. For example, go up the snakes and down the ladders, teach them to experiment and see what happens.

* Teach and encourage older children to **design** and **invent**, for example, a mobile, a robot, pop-up books. Children have great **imagination** for inventing things - encourage it.

* Encourage young writers to make a family monthly **magazine**, a class magazine, a school magazine, a club magazine for all their friends and neighbours.

* Encourage outside **communications** and relationships, let them write to far off family members, pen pals, encourage 'thank you' cards (homemade) for presents received. And homemade gifts for birthdays and Christmas that they have to put some thought and effort into making.

* Try to link things and happenings to their everyday lives. How the general election may affect us. How the European parliament decisions affect farmers and therefore our milk supply. How everyday things we do like using plastic bags effect the environment, our world.

* Encourage them to participate in local clubs, or television clubs or **organisations** like EARTHWATCH or AMNESTY INTERNATIONAL.

* Encourage the interest and love of **music** by playing all different kinds of music on a regular basis. Let them experiment with sounds, and as they grow older watch out for sounds and instruments they like and ask if they would like to play a particular instrument and arrange lessons if you possibly can.

* For ten minutes to half an hour each day (depending on your child's age) have a **learning session**. Pick a comfortable place in your home where you are not disturbed. Have a good supply of writing materials, scrap paper, pens, crayons, glue, different materials or cut-outs and reading materials. Don't try to do too much at each session - make it fun and end it on a happy note before boredom levels are reached.

* **Mathematics** can be difficult for some children - make it a fun subject by visualising it, use shapes, telling the time, memorising tables to music.

* Always keep involved with you child's **school life**, always know what is going on, involve yourself in school functions, parent associations etc.

* Listening, talking, laughing and working out things together can be educational and fun for both parent and child.

* **Don't compare** your children with others, it is always counter-productive. Accept them as they are with their own special talents.

* **Homework** need not be a drag if they are motivated into wanting to know more.

* Encourage **time alone** for thinking, reading, and learning from a very early age. This will develop into a pattern of life they will continue.

* Do not disturb them at these solitary learning times so they develop the ability to **concentrate**.

* Be careful not to over-correct or insist on perfection - it does not matter if they are not so good at maths, they may be great at English, don't over-emphasise weaknesses. Make sure you balance any negatives out with how good they are at other things to encourage a **good self-image**.

* Remember that children learn by example, so keep your mind open and fresh to **new ideas** too.

* Always remember that a balance of love, security, study and play makes for a healthy happy mind.

* Finally, ask yourself what do you really what for your child? Being highly intelligent may be an asset but having a child who is happy and knows how to enjoy life and appreciate the miracle of each day is more important. There is no harm in letting them have the wealth of intelligence as well, so long as we keep it in the right perspective.

First steps
in reading

If you look closely at children around two years, they want to learn and are curious about everything - to the point that they may drive their parents to distraction. A very young child can learn how to read words and sentences just the way they learn to speak. The information is soaked up like a sponge; she can learn to read easily and naturally and should be given the opportunity to do so. Reading is not a chore, it is a fun thing to do. Start off positively - learning is a great adventure. Only well behaved children should be given the exciting opportunity to play the reading game. Keep the reading and game short but fun.

Before * Read to your baby regularly from birth.
reading * Encourage a love of **books**. When you read together
               cuddle up close so warmth, love, security and pleasure
               become associated with books

* Have plenty of books around the house.

* Let reading and learning be a fun game.

* Any learning sessions should always end before the child
   wants to stop.

* Make use of your local **library**.

* Play with familiar **rhymes**. Say 'Jack and Jill went up the
   lane' and they'll correct you.

* **Rhyme games**: what rhymes with cat, mat, hat, Bill, hill,
   will.

* **Listening game**: with closed eyes, guess the noise of
   closing a door, clapping a hand.

* **Memory game**: place a few objects on a tray and remove
   one - guess which one.

* **Grouping and matching**: sorting out socks, spoons,
   shoes, beans, playing shop.

* Encourage **observations** in the shops - talk about colour,
   shapes, size, hot, cold.

* Use full instructions, **don't baby talk**. 'Please get me the
   red book, from the table in the hall.'

* Through these activities and games a child absorbs and
   practices the skill of **language**.

Reading tips   * Choose **suitable books** with a decent size print and well spaced out words, with pictures that clearly match the words and have a strong story line.

* Make **reading cards** on stiff white card four inches high. Start with words like Mummy and Daddy, go on to 'self-words', for example, nose, eyes, leg, leading to words in your child's immediate world like chair, toy.

* Simply introduce a card until the child knows it (it could take one day or one week) and go on to the next word. Make it fun.

* Remember the supreme rule of **never boring** the child!

* Choose a time when you are both relaxed and can give it your full attention.

* Don't get anxious. That takes the joy of it away.

* With books just run your finger under the line of print slowly.

* Pick out **key words** like dog. Emphasise them in word and in the picture.

* Suggest they read the story with you next time.

* **Read slowly.** They may only remember one word, it's a start. Adjust your speed to their pace, and practice.

* Give time to look at the **picture** and remember the **words.**

* Don't insist they read every word correctly, go back and read together later to correct a mistake.

* When reading together, gradually drop out for a few words, then a few sentences if they cope well reading alone.

* If they forget a word give a **clue**, Sshh - for ship.

* **Cards** can be placed on common objects in the home, table, chair, door.

* Have **word days,** today's word is shoe. Build up vocabulary like this.

* Do **praise** and build **confidence** up. Make them believe they can do it.

* **Be patient.** Take it at your child's pace.

* Don't expect quick results, expect slow progress at the beginning.

Accidents and first aid

Accidents are part of growing up - even the most carefully watched and loved children will have mishaps at some stage of childhood. But knowing what to do makes a parent feel calmer and more in control, which will reassure an upset or hurt child. Also it is important to have some idea of what complications could occur. Generally for the little bumps, minor knocks and bruises always give praise for bravery. We as a whole family 'wish it better' together, encouraging children to believe they can heal themselves. Use lovely coloured plasters they can show off with pride. Also a bandage or an 'ouch' sign taped to a child's clothes will make them feel important and discourage touches in the sensitive area. You could also teach relaxing and breathing techniques to help relieve pain and calm down an upset child. Keep a book (like this) or a first aid manual near to your first aid box for little emergencies, so you can look it up and not just panic.

Bruises and bumps
* Bruises are caused by bleeding underneath the skin.
* Apply a flannel wrapped around ice cubes to allay the **swelling** of big bumps (within the first twenty-four hours or as soon as possible).
* Later, warm heat applied to a **bruise** may speed recovery.
* An ice lolly or ice-cream given after a **bruised lip** is a good soother and reduces swelling.
* The inside of a banana skin is good for a **black eye**.
* Have a small plastic bag of uncooked rice frozen in the freezer for a good **compress** that can accommodate any shape of bump.

Cuts and grazes
* If a **severe cut**, press firmly on the wound with a clean pad until bleeding stops. This may take five to ten minutes.
* Lay the child down and **raise the injured limb** provided it is not broken.
* If a **small cut**, wash your hands, and run cut under a slow trickle of tepid water. Remove any dirt or debris with a clean piece of gauze. A mild antiseptic can be used if you like.
* **Cover with a plaster or dressing** and leave on for two to three days to heal.
* If cuts are severe call an ambulance - if the accident occurred outside, ask doctor about a **tetanus injection**.

Stings and bites	*	The skin's normal response to a sting or bite is to swell, redden, then itch.
	*	**Remove** any visible sting with tweezers.
	*	Keep one of the commercial products to treat. Alternatively, the following **households remedies** work well. Apply: cold compress and calamine lotion; wet soap or toothpaste; baking soda and water (especially useful for treating wasp stings); spit (at least you're never without this); vinegar to a bee sting.
	*	Occasionally a child or adult has a severe **allergic reaction** (anaphylactic) to a sting. Symptoms may include shock, a rash, fever or exhaustion. If any of these symptoms occur, seek medical attention.
	*	All large animal or human **bites** should be shown to a doctor, as these are more likely to cause infection.
Scalds and burns (minor)	*	**Cool skin** as quickly as possible by gently holding under running cold water for ten minutes.
	*	Take off jewellery or tight belts etc, as the skin swells up quickly.
	*	If clothes stick to skin, don't touch them.
	*	**Cover** with a sterile, dry, non-fluffy dressing.
	*	Don't put any substance on a burn - leave it alone.
	*	If the area affected is large, call for an **ambulance**.
Choking	*	Don't try to pick object out, unless it's very easy to get hold of.
	*	Hold baby or child **upside down** and **slap** smartly between shoulder blades. Repeat if necessary.
	*	As a last resort give the child's tummy a short sharp squeeze to push the object out of the windpipe. Support the child's back with one hand, clench your fist and press it into the abdomen using quick, upward, inward pressure to dislodge blockage.

Foreign bodies

Nose	*	Close off the other nostril and tell child to blow out hard - if this doesn't work, don't poke around, go to Casualty.
Ear	*	Objects may be removed with tweezers, but this is potentially dangerous - leave to the doctor if too far in.
	*	An insect in the ear can be floated out if you pour warm water in.

Eye * Objects can be dislodged by water - so for once, **bawling crying** is actively encouraged. Alternatively, **immerse** side of face in a basin of water.

* Do not let them rub or touch the eye.

* Gently use the tip of damp cotton wool (or cotton bud) to **remove particle.**

* If unsuccessful, cover with pad and go straight to **Casualty.** Don't mess around with eyes.

* If damaging fluid has got into eyes, again use plenty of cool water, cover and go to hospital.

Nose bleeds * Nose bleeds look and feel upsetting but are rarely dangerous. Reassure, lean child forward, pinch the middle of the nose for five minutes.

* If they happen frequently they may have a weak blood vessel that needs cauterising. See your GP.

Broken bones * Keep child warm, and be reassuring.

* Call the doctor or ambulance

* Don't move the child unless you have to.

* Don't give the child anything to eat or drink.

* Splint, pad and support if necessary but ideally it's better to wait for medical aid.

Poisoning * If you think your child has swallowed or eaten something bad **go to hospital immediately.**

* Take the suspect container with you if possible.

* Gently give milk or water to drink to dilute if caustic chemicals were taken.

* Time is of the essence. Don't hang around.

When you need to take your child to hospital after an accident * If they have been **unconscious** at all.

* If their **pupil size** is unequal.

* If they are **vomiting** or **drowsy.**

* If they are **bleeding from the ears.**

* If they have **stopped breathing at any stage.**

* If they have **lost a lot of blood.**

* If they have a lot of **pain** somewhere.

Parents can learn about First Aid from the RED CROSS or ST JOHN'S AMBULANCE.

Safety first

Before we have children, we don't realise the potential dangers around. All sorts of lethal appliances and sharp objects seem to be just everywhere. All homes need adjustments to make them childproof. Take time to discuss and consider potential hazards that exist for children at home and in daily routines. Minor accidents are part of growing up, and can't be avoided, but it is important to teach children to recognise dangers around them. Prevent accidents and protect children by using safety equipment, for example fireguards and car seat-belts. Remember too that accidents tend to happen in times of stress, when you're in a hurry. So take care! And teach them to do the same.

Safety tips
* Get **organised**. A tidy person will not have to reorganise their home too much but untidy types like me must make a big effort to clear up - don't leave dangerous plastic bags, electrical appliances or poisonous fluids lying around.

* **Never, not even for a second, leave your child alone** in a potentially dangerous situation, for example in the bath, on a changing unit, near water or whilst eating.

* Always put a **harness** on the baby in a high chair, push chair or pram.

* Once your baby can **crawl**, go around your house on your hands and knees and look at your house from the child's point of view - then adjust it.

* Always put the cold water into the bath first, never the hot. And use a **safety mat** to avoid slips.

* Buy **fire resistant clothes** for children and don't dry clothes on a fireguard.

* Don't leave pins, buttons or beads around the house.

* Don't give peanuts to young children.

* Be watchful of open-weave acrylic cardigans or clothes with threads or ribbons. They can hook onto something and choke baby.

* Keep **sharp objects** out of children's reach.

* Get into the habit of turning pan handles inwards. Keep hot drinks away from toddlers, especially when you are drinking at the table. Be careful with used ashtrays.

* Do not give babies **pillows**. Don't put a cot near a window or furniture that can be climbed onto.

* Make sure **flexes** do not trail around. Remove flex-knots or tape them, so little fingers cannot pull them.

* **Medicines** and **poisonous substances** should be kept out of reach, preferably in a locked cupboard. Paint the tops of all dangerous fluids with red nail varnish, so you can teach children red means danger.

* Children can fall from stairs, windows, trees, fences and balconies. Use stair-gates and window locks where possible, and have no-go areas.

* Children can **drown** in a few inches of water. Tell them about the danger teach them how to **swim** at an early age.

* Windows or **glass** doors can be a great danger. Use toughened or laminated glass for low or large areas of glass. You can also get special plastic film for glass. If glass cracks, a wet piece of kitchen roll should be used to pick up small splinters. Put transfers up at child-level to remind them that it's not just open space.

* Let children use **unbreakable cups**, and put them within easy reach on a low shelf.

* The thermostat on your hot water system should be no higher than 54C.

* **Night lights** are a good idea.

* Don't let children walk or run while holding anything in their mouth, like a lollipop or pencil.

* **Don't use table cloths** when young children are around.

* Put **high bolts** on the doors of dangerous rooms and keep little ones out.

* Teach them not to slam doors - young fingers are easily trapped.

* Teach **road safety**!

* Always insist on children wearing proper **restrainers** in the car. Never leave any child unattended in a car.

* Check all **toys** and **equipment** regularly for safety.

* Do have a 'safety' chat with any others staying at your house, especially the elderly who tend to leave pills lying around, or workers that children may be fascinated by - watch out for them handling saws or nails.

* Make **safety rules** for your children, keep them simple and explain the reasons behind them.

Minor infectious illnesses
of childhood

Most children get at least one infectious illness at some stage, although measles, mumps and Rubella are getting less common now children are being vaccinated against them. So if you can, immunise. However, they may still catch a slight version of the infection without the severe symptoms. It is well worth having your own clinical thermometer handy. You should keep your thermometer in a glass jar containing a weak antiseptic solution. Before use, rinse in cold water and give it a little shake. Normal temperature taken under the tongue is 36.9C, lower if the temperature is taken under the child's arm. Card-type thermometers are also very useful as they are very easy to read. If a toddler has a high temperature, sponge the child down with cool water, to prevent fitting, and keep the child lightly clad and the room temperature low. If this doesn't bring the temperature down, seek medical advice.

Measles * Cold-like symptoms and white grain-like spots inside child's mouth. On the third day pink spots appear behind the ears and the face, gradually spreading all over, temperature rising with rash. Symptoms appear eight to ten days after being exposed to infection. Measles is particularly infectious just prior to rash and can lead to serious complications. Avoid exposure to cold or draughts and pay special attention to eyes, ears and mouth. Complete recovery takes between two and four weeks. A homoeopathic remedy is pulsatilla.

Whooping cough * Starts with heavy cold, persistent cough and temperature. Cough worsens and becomes explosive, worst at night. Can include vomiting. Symptoms begin within eight to fourteen days after exposure. Keep child in bed and call a doctor. Feed small meals after coughing bouts and give plenty of fluids. Taking the child daily into a steam-filled bathroom can help soothe cough. Serious lung complications can occur. Whooping cough can last three weeks or more. A homoeopathic remedy is Drosera.

Mumps * Starts with a temperature and a general feeling of being unwell, stiffness and pain in neck and jaw lead to swelling of face and neck. Vomiting sometimes occurs. Mumps develop three weeks after exposure. Keep the child warm and call a doctor. Give plenty of drinks. A homoeopathic remedy is Pulsatilla.

Chicken pox * Starts with vague upset, temperature and headache. Rash of small red marks, initially on back, chest or stomach and spreading all over. The rash is itchy and can scar. Can occur in mouth, which is painful. Spots become blisters then crust. Give fluids and ice cream etc. Apply calamine lotion or witch hazel to soothe. Be careful of transmitting shingles (caused by the same virus) to the elderly. Symptoms start three weeks after exposure, keep isolated until all rash gone. Chicken pox lasts about two weeks. A homoeopathic remedy is Rhus tox.

Scarlet fever * Starts with temperature and fever. Sometimes vomiting occurs, and a sore throat or fur-coated tongue is followed by very red tongue, leading to a bright red rash over all the body for two or three days (not on face). Symptoms start after three days. Call your doctor, antibiotics usually help. Give plenty of fluids. Oral hygiene is important - use a mouthwash.

Rubella / German measles * Getting less common now, symptoms include a mild rash, pink spots, slight fever and slight joint pains. Inform your doctor and isolate child until rash has cleared. Keep away from pregnant women as Rubella causes serious complications to unborn babies in first four months of pregnancy.

Tonsillitis * Sore throat, white spots on tonsils, headache, general aches and pains and high temperature. It is common between the ages of four to eight years. Call your GP if symptoms last more than two or three days or if temperature rises very high - antibiotics may be needed. Homoeopathic remedy for influenza-type symptoms is Gelsemium.

Rash guide

Children can produce all shapes and sizes of rashes that can come and go quite suddenly. Some accompany an illness (see Infectious Illnesses), others can be the result of sensitivity, for example to heat, or allergic reactions to foods.

Cradle cap * Thick yellow scales of skin on the scalp of the very young baby: soak in olive oil overnight, wash gently, and dry with circular movements to dislodge scales.

Urticaria Neonatorum * Newborn baby's skin becomes blotchy red, maybe with white spots. Should disappear in a couple of days without any treatment.

Scabies * Itchy pimples with tiny black spots, often found between fingers or groin. Look for a furrow line of the mite. See GP - needs medication.

Ringworm * A circle of small white bumps surrounded by reddened area, or a grey scaly ring on any place on the body - it is contagious, so see your GP. Needs anti-fungal cream.

Milia * White spots on nose or cheeks of newborn. Do not touch, will just disappear.

Thrush * White milky flecks on inside of cheeks and tongue. If you brush them away they leave raw patches. Can also cause a persistent nappy rash. Suspect thrush if all home treatments fail on nappy rash.

Hives * Itchy white lumps on a red background - can be tiny or large swollen white patches, can disappear to be replaced by another crop. Usually a skin reaction to foodstuffs like strawberries, or medicines such as penicillin. Usually the cause is plain old nettle rash if summertime.

Eczema * Dry, itchy, sore rash found commonly behind ears or on face, neck and the creases of the body. Can get open and sore, even crack and cause a discharge. Thought to be an allergic response and often associated with asthma. Skin needs intensive care and moisturising (see section on **Eczema**).

Heat rash * A faint red rash over the neck, face and trunk, especially heavy around skin creases giving a generally flushed appearance. Sponge down with cool water to remove sweat from the body, then keep cool if possible and keep out of the sun.

Purpura * A very important rash to recognise, purple-red rash of irregular spidery spots which do not itch, and stay if you press them. This is really bleeding underneath the skin and can be caused by a number of diseases. It can be a reaction to a new medication or a simple infection. But it can indicate something much more serious, for example hepatitis, leukaemia, or it could indicate meningitis if accompanied by a high fever, so definitely one to check out with your doctor.

What to do * Generally soothe itchy rashes with calamine lotion or cold compresses. A bath of lukewarm water containing a handful of bread soda eases itch. For a homoeopathic remedy, try Merc Sol.

* Discourage scratching, use cotton mittens if necessary. Teach child to press and rub instead, keep well occupied to distract.

* Keep child as cool as possible - over-heating usually makes matters worse.

* Find out allergen and remove the cause of sensitivity if possible.

* If rash is accompanied by fever or is persistent, seek medical advice.

Constipation

A baby or child is not constipated simply because they have not had a bowel action for a couple of days. The definition of constipation is when hard stools are passed with obvious difficulty. So if your child has not had a bowel action for a few days and then passes small stone-like stools, then s/he is constipated.

Symptoms of constipation

* No bowel action for days followed by obvious discomfort and straining.

* When passed, small stone-like hard pieces of faeces.

* Blood or mucus passed with hard stools.

* Just keep in mind that everybody has their own pattern of bowel movements, and what may be normal for one child is not necessarily the norm for all children. So constipation without any other signs of illness is not necessarily anything to worry about. Left to themselves our bowels will just empty automatically by reflex when full, so if constipation occurs, diet is normally responsible. If constipation recurs, consult your GP.

When and why constipation occurs

* It is common that following an illness a child may not have a proper bowel motion for a few days, often this is simply because the child has not eaten much.

* Constipation may be caused by a loss of fluids from the body - eg after a high temperature, or during hot weather.

* When a baby is introduced to solid food at the beginning of the weaning process constipation may occur.

* If your child for whatever reason becomes tense, this could prevent the relaxation needed to pass a motion. This may happen during potty training, the whole process may be making your child tense, even upset. Ease up for a few days. Make the training fun, not something to get 'uptight' over.

Relieving * Increase the child's **clear fluid** intake.
constipation * Add an extra ounce of water to the baby's bottle each
feed time.

* Give extra boiled water in between feeds, you could even
add a half teaspoon of prune juice.

* Give **diluted fruit juice** mid-morning or in the afternoon.

* A half teaspoon of sugar added to the fruit juice may help
relieve constipation although some experts claim it gives
babies a sweet tooth. I'm not convinced, my advice would
be that sugar helps your child, that half a teaspoon
occasionally will not make your child a sugar addict.

* Once baby is on a mixed diet, **stewed prunes** can be
given. Mix them with ice-cream if the baby takes them
better.

* Encourage older children to take lots of pure fruit drinks
(especially prune) and lots of extra water.

* Ensure your child's diet contains lots of **fresh produce**,
fruit and root vegetables, wholemeal products, brown
breads, pastas and brown rice.

* Cut out processed foods and increase unprocessed foods.

* **Green vegetables** and **root vegetables** help. Add honey
to the cooking water if you must to sweeten them up,
most children like honeyed sprouts or carrots.

* Put a little Vaseline on the opening of your child's back
passage if it is sore to pass a hard motion.

* Ensure that the toilet or potty your child uses is
comfortable. Most big toilets don't suit little soft
bottoms, use a potty or buy a small seat to fit into the
larger toilet seat. Perhaps sitting nearby when your child
uses the toilet or potty may help relaxation.

* Try these steps first then go to your doctor should you
need to. Do not use laxatives or suppositories without
consulting your GP first.

* If your child has developed a chronic constipation
problem your doctor may prescribe a relaxant medicine if
your child is 'uptight' about the whole procedure.

* Finally try not to get obsessive about your child's bowel
habits as this always leads to trouble. If the right diet is
given and enough fluids in a healthy environment with
plenty of fresh air and exercise, a bowel will respond by
emptying when full without your worrying about it.

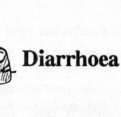

Diarrhoea

If your baby has very watery stools and they are a funny colour, maybe green, and very smelly, or if your baby is generally ill, not eating and has a temperature then you should see a doctor straight away. This is dangerous diarrhoea and could even be gastro-enteritis which can lead to severe dehydration and even death if left untreated long enough. If young babies get diarrhoea and seem sickly with it, it is always best to check it out. However, the diarrhoea children contract is most often the milder form caused by eating the wrong foods, so if your child has diarrhoea with no other symptoms we can usually find out the cause ourselves and take steps to relieve it. If diarrhoea still continues, a doctor should be consulted, as otherwise dehydration can set in. Signs of dehydration are dry mouth, infrequent passing of water, fever, dry skin, dark rings under the child's eyes and, when pinched, a skin fold fails to sink down. A child with these symptoms needs immediate medical attention.

Possible causes of diarrhoea	* If **breastfeeding**, the mother's diet may need to be revised to see if any food eaten could have caused the upset. For example too much fruit in the mother's diet.

* If **bottle feeding**, check out your sterilisation technique to ensure it is adequate.

* The diarrhoea may be caused by another illness, infection or virus such as **tonsillitis** or **otitis media** (ear infection) - have your GP check for an underlying sickness.

* **Teething** can often cause a loose, acidic stool. Be extremely vigilant changing nappies, otherwise nappy rash will ensue.

* When introducing new foods at weaning time only introduce one new taste at a time, or the bowel may become irritated. Introducing one new food at time also makes it easier to identify allergies.

* Once they are mobile, young toddlers tend to put everything in their mouth and diarrhoea may be the result of a germ they have picked up.

* Be extra careful with baby's food in summer time - never reheat food or leave it out where flies can get at it. All these things could lead to a child getting infected food, leading to diarrhoea. Check your **hygiene** measures in the kitchen.

* Over feeding can cause diarrhoea.

* Be wary of **cold meats** and **prepared foods** as these could be potential sources of **food poisoning.**

* If travelling, drink only **bottled water.**

* Give half strength feeds for a day, by using half the regular formula to the same amount of water.

* With a toddler stop all food and give **clear fluids only** for twenty-four hours. For example water and diluted fruit juices with a pinch of salt and spoonful of sugar, boiled lemonade, or even flat cola.

* When reintroducing the food, start with non-dairy products, for example stewed apples or sieved vegetables, mashed potatoes or mashed bananas. Avoid milky things and meat for a few days more.

* Only offer small amounts of food, but frequently, until appetite returns to normal.

* By the fourth day normal feeding can be resumed, all going well.

* If the diarrhoea comes back a bit when food is re-introduced, the fluid diet may be continued for another day but after that a doctor needs to be consulted. A specially prescribed glucose and salt mixture may be necessary to ensure the fluid and electrolyte balance in the body is maintained.

* Do be careful about **hygiene** at this time so the diarrhoea does not spread to the whole family.

* Always encourage the child with diarrhoea to drink lots of fluids.

* A **home-made binder** can be given when re-introducing food again in the form of water in which rice has been boiled, then the rice itself given with stewed fruit to make it taste nice.

* Do not give the commercial anti-diarrhoea medicines to a child under five years old without first talking to your doctor.

The common cold

Both adults and children may suffer from this dreaded illness as soon as winter comes upon us. So what exactly is it? In fact it is not one but many and varied viruses that are caught literally from the air when other people sneeze or breathe on us. Because it is caused by so many different viruses, anti-viral agents and antibiotics are of no use unless a secondary infection is caught. We are more susceptible to getting colds if we are run down, very young, very old, or under a lot of strain which parents of young children usually are, so we are all prime targets. But there are many practical ways of trying to prevent infection and of limiting the severity of a cold, although at present there is no actual cure.

Tips to help the common cold

* If perhaps we are run down, or have been having sleepless nights at home with our darling children, or out celebrating, our immune system will not be working efficiently. So get as much **rest** as you can - eat a **healthy diet** with lots of fresh fruit and vegetables (raw if possible). Drink plenty of fluids.

* In winter give children extra **Vitamin C and cod liver oil** capsules.

* Teach children how to blow their nose properly from an early age. Teach them to cover each nostril, one at a time, with a handkerchief in hand and blow out of the other nostril.

* Put Vaseline around nostrils to prevent them getting sore.

* Use a cotton bud to clear the excess mucus from just inside the lower nostril of a baby.

* Cut down on dairy produce as it is mucus-forming.

* Vitamins which especially help to improve our body's defense system are: **Vitamin A**, found in carrots, apricots, liver and watercress; **Folic acid**, found in brewer's yeast and tuna fish; **Zinc**, found in peanuts, egg yolk, whole grains and beans (encourage the old brown bread and peanut butter sandwich).

* A **garlic clove** a day is not just thought to ward off evil spirits but colds too. You can buy them in capsules to save those with sensitive noses from knowing you take them. Or just splash out on garlicky pasta or salad dishes and enjoy protecting yourself!

* If your baby or child develops a temperature and is suffering from aches and pains use **paracetamol syrups** without added sugar to relieve the symptoms.

* For a sore throat suck **boiled sweets** or medicated throat **pastilles** or **gargle with a weak solution of salt** (my father's remedy for many ills).

* Catarrh may be helped by a **decongestant spray** or for children use the small capsules which you can break and put the fluid on their pillow at night to relieve the blockage and congestion.

* Also to relieve that 'blocked up feeling' use old fashioned **steam inhalation** - fill a small basin with water and a few menthol crystals or friar's balsam, or use vapour rub.

* For adults, at the first sign of a cold coming, drink a cup of **hot water** with the juice of a **lemon** and a teaspoon of **honey**, a large pinch of **cayenne pepper** or **whiskey**, both will give your system the jolt it may need. You may even enjoy it!

* **Elderflower tea** is a good cold remedy which works, use a teaspoon of flowers per cup (or 1 oz to a pint) of boiling water, leave twenty minutes to infuse. Then drink it last thing at night. Add honey and ginger to taste.

* **Camphorated oil** rubbed on the chest relieves chestiness.

* Don't forget that a day or two cuddled up with a **hot water bottle** may give you a well deserved rest time.

* Drink plenty of **fluids**.

* Watch for **earache** complications in young children, especially toddlers. They wake at night, screaming and pulling their ears. Take them to the GP if you suspect this.

* Adults can take extra **Vitamin C** to fight colds.

* Finally, do still get plenty of **fresh air**. Staying in stuffy rooms can make a cold heavy and unbearable.

* **Homoeopathic remedies** for colds are: **Aconite** for sudden onset after exposure to cold. **Gelsemium** for flu-like symptoms, aches and pains. **Nat Mur** for sneeze colds and nose running like a tap.

Eczema

Eczema is a very annoying and upsetting skin condition. It is a dry, red, scaly, irritable skin condition that can manifest itself in various ways. In a baby it can appear as little red patches on cheeks, forehead or bottom. As the child gets older the patches are commonly found on the hands, wrists, ankles, and at the back of the ears and knees, and generally in the creases of the skin. When it's bad it can look like little cuts or cracks on the skin which can get weepy and wet. It can really be trying when it is severe, causing extreme itchiness that can be unbearable, which keeps the baby crying and unsettled day and night. No one is sure exactly what causes eczema but there is a definite link to allergies, asthma and hayfever. The risk of developing eczema is increased if there is a history or background of allergies in the family. Eczema usually flares up in a baby at around three to twelve months. After that it waxes and wanes throughout toddler life but usually 90% of eczema has disappeared by the time the child starts school.

What to do about eczema

* If there is a history of allergies in the family, especially eczema, asthma, hayfever, find out what the **allergens** are and avoid them throughout pregnancy, and then consider avoiding them in the first few years of your baby's life, if possible.

* If the **family history** of these conditions is severe think about getting in touch with FORESIGHT (Pre-conceptual Care Association - address listed at the back of this book) for ways to try to avoid passing these allergies on to the next generation.

* **Breastfeed** your baby for as long as you can, even a short time would be beneficial. The breastfeeding mother should also avoid any of the common allergens found in the family's history.

* Avoid substances that make the eczema worse. For example, you may have to cut out all dairy products, or avoid chemical additives and preservatives, especially artificial colourants agents.

* If an allergy is suspected your GP may help you track down the allergen that has started off the eczema

* The **diet** may need to be revised by a **process of elimination.** For young children, this process should be carried out under supervision, to make sure your child is not missing out on essential vitamins or minerals.

* An **aluminium toxicity** was found in some eczema sufferers so aluminium cookware may be best avoided.

* Common food allergens are **wheat, eggs** and **dairy produce,** including cow's milk.

* Do be careful when **introducing solid food** to baby, especially if allergies are in the family. Give each new food separately and wait two days before introducing another food to see if the first causes any reaction.

* **Soya-based formulae** can be used as a substitute for regular formula milk for babies if the baby does have a milk allergy.

* Recent research found that eczema sufferers were often deficient in essential fatty acids. **Evening Primrose Oil** helped to reduce the itching, encouraging a healthier sleeping pattern. For example, for adults four to six 500mgs capsules of Evening Primrose Oil (two or three times daily), and for children two to three years old one daily, four to five years old two daily, over seven years four daily. The Evening Primrose Oil Caps 250 mgs may be an easier size for children to swallow so double the above number of capsules. It is also available as fluid in a dropper bottle for the very young and is available on prescription as well as over the counter at many chemists. To get the optimum use of the essential fatty acid you could also take **Vitamin B6, Vitamin C** and **Zinc** tablets.

Skin care * Keep the skin **moisturised** at all times, even hourly if necessary when the eczema is severe.

* Keep the skin **clean**, dirt itches.

* When eczema is severe, bath daily. Some children's eczema may improve with bathing, though in some cases it may make it worse. Generally sponge rather than bathe if it makes the eczema worse.

* Add **oil** to bath, for example emulsiderm, oilatum.

* When severe, use emulsifying ointment in bath.

* Vitamin E oil can be combined with Vaseline for a good spreading healing moisturiser.

* Calamine lotion can be used to heal and soothe sore areas.

* **Do not use soap** or bubble bath.

* After the bath pat the skin dry - **do not rub.** Then dab on the ointments and/or moisturisers as needed.

* Your doctor can prescribe **anti-histamine** syrups to

relieve the itching and help the child to sleep if the eczema is disturbing sleep patterns.

* Teach the child not to **scratch**, but to rub, squeeze or press instead.

* Put **cotton mittens** on the young baby.

* Use **cotton** or cotton-mix clothes only and keep them loose. Tight or woollen type clothes can itch like mad.

* Use terry nappies with liners as they itch less than disposables. Rinse the wash very well.

* Eczema gets worse in the **winter** - always keep the hands covered with gloves.

* **Central heating** can make it worse, keep a **bowl of water** in the rooms to moisturise the air. Some parents use spring water spray mists to keep the skin moist and it is very refreshing.

* When washing clothes avoid the low temperature biological enzyme powders, avoid perfumed conditioners, bleaches, and **rinse** clothes well.

* Make all this extra washing and skin care fun - get lots of toys for the bath, let children draw things on themselves with the creams.

* **Avoid sand play** - it can aggravate the condition.

* It can be very tiring having a baby with this condition. Get lots of support and rest as much as you can, to help you cope with night time wakings.

* The toddler with all this itching gets extra frustrated and tantrums are inevitable. Get some time to yourself. Get a patient babysitter so you can recharge your patience batteries (know your PARENTS UNDER STRESS or CRYSIS phone numbers (see the back of this book)

* Some parents have found acupuncture, reflexology, Chinese herbal teas and treatments, and other complementary medicine treatments helpful.

* **Homoeopathic remedies** may help. Gunpowder 6. 1 dose morning and evening may help for chronic eczema or Ars Alb 6, 1 dose three times daily for very dry skin. Graphites, if the skin is cracked and weeping. But it may be best to get individual counselling from a homeopath so they can give the perfect remedy to suit your child's skin condition.

* Finally join the nearest ECZEMA SOCIETY, addresses at the back of this book.

Your family doctor

Having a good general practitioner is a must for all parents. We must be able to feel we can trust our doctor and feel s/he is sympathetic to our family's needs. Try your best to get to know your doctor's working routines so you know the best time to call for advice. Ask would s/he mind you telephoning about things you are unsure of, and find out what the situation is regarding home calls. Shop around for a different doctor if you must. As a mother myself I feel that instinctively a parent knows when there is something wrong with a baby and a good doctor knows this too, and listens to you carefully. It could be that you may read this list of when to call a doctor and your child or baby's symptoms are not listed. It may be that your child is just acting differently, very quiet, or listless when usually boisterous. So what do you do, maybe it is a difficult time to call the doctor, you do not like to seem an over-anxious parent. My advice is this, only a person who is very close to the child (that's you) can pick up the warning signs of sickness and if you are worried or in doubt at all contact your doctor. It may only be necessary for the doctor to reassure you on the telephone. But your guideline should always be when in doubt ask, and in general the younger the child the more important it is to seek help.

When to call your doctor and what to say

Pain
* If a child has **continuous head or stomach pain.**
* If a fall results in **blurred vision** or any **loss of consciousness.**
* If a headache is accompanied by **sickness** or **dizziness.**
* If your child complains of **any severe pain** which is **repeated at regular intervals.**

Temperature
* If a baby's **temperature** rises above 101F (38C) and your baby is obviously ill.
* If a baby's temperature is above 103F (39.5C) and your baby doesn't seem ill.
* If a high temperature rises by more than 2 degrees.
* If the temperature is fluctuating and gradually rising.
* If the temperature does not come down even though you take measures such as **tepid sponging, paracetamol syrup,** and clothe the baby only in a vest and nappy.
* If the child has a **stiff neck** and **headache** with the fever.

* If the baby starts having **febrile convulsions**.

* If the high temperature lasts more than **three days**.

* If your baby feels **cold to touch**, is **drowsy, listless** and **limp**. In the case of **hypothermia** the baby's hands, limbs and face can appear fine.

Breathing * If breathing is obviously **painful**, or if your child is labouring and can't get enough air or if your baby is having to suck in deeply, bringing in the lower ribs.

* If your baby **stops breathing** and **changes colour** (the exception is the breath holding attacks that can happen as part of a tantrum with toddlers).

* Very **noisy** breathing.

Vomiting * If vomiting and diarrhoea persist and clearly the child is
and losing more fluid than s/he can take in. This can cause
diarrhoea rapid **dehydration** and is very dangerous, especially for young babies.

* If vomiting is severe or prolonged or accompanied by **pain** or **temperature**.

* If diarrhoea is continuous or causing **pain** or high **temperature**.

Others * **Earache** that keeps a child awake, irritable and crying.

* **Blood passed**, in the form of saliva, vomit, phlegm (except nose bleeds).

* If a young baby under six months consistently **stops taking bottles**.

* Any **accident, burn** or **knock** that you are worried about.

* When an **accidental wound** is deep or results in a large blood loss.

* If your child gets **bitten** by an animal, human, or snake (OK it is rare but I know of one child who was bitten by a snake who was a pet, and another who was bitten by some weird exotic bird - oh there's never a dull moment with kids around!)

* Consult your doctor if **chemicals** ever get in your **child's eyes**, or if the eye looks damaged at all.

Tips to get the most from your doctor

* Make an **appointment** if you can.

* Get **organised** before you phone - have a pen and paper ready, write down all the symptoms and when they started. Note your child's temperature, breathing, eating, vomiting, bowel movement, any medication she is on, or anything else relevant (if you go on a visit take this list with you too).

* Mention what you think the problem could be, and anything that may be happening at home that may be relevant. Exams, family disputes, school problems, emotional problems can affect health.

* Find out and make a note of both family medical histories if available, for example allergies, heart disease, diabetes.

* If you think your child may have an **infectious** disease, phone first. The doctor may prefer to visit you or might ask you to call after surgery hours.

* Talk to your children about doctors and how they look after sick people. Introduce them as caring, friendly people. Encourage them to like the doctor, explain what the doctor might do. For example, s/he might look into your ears, listen to your chest, and so on (see the recommended book list).

* Do not go to your doctor with every cold but if you are worried, phone to ease your mind. Reassuring advice may be all you need. No good doctor should mind being asked for advice.

* Make a **list of questions** you want to ask and be satisfied you have had them all answered before you leave.

* If **medication** or **instructions** are given, make sure you understand all about it. Are there any side effects? When do you give it and how often? Can a normal diet be taken?

* If you have visited your doctor several times with the same illness and don't seem to be getting anywhere, ask for a second opinion or to be referred to a **specialist**.

* Don't be put off if you are told the doctor is busy, simply ask when would it be a convenient time to talk.

* Do not be afraid of your doctor. S/he would rather have you leave the surgery satisfied and reassured, than upset because you are frightened to ask another question.

* Remember too that advice on diet, lifestyle and hygiene can be just as important as getting medication sometimes.

Allergies

What is an allergy? Well, when a healthy child's body comes into contact with germs the body makes antibodies to fight off the offending germ. A child with an allergy is sensitive to substances that are not germs, but these substances or allergens cause the body to react in various ways as if it were being invaded by germs. This is called an allergic reaction. Three classic allergies are asthma, eczema and hay fever. Allergies seem to be on the increase. Research has found that more than 20% of children are affected by one allergic disorder before they become teenagers and 2% of newborn babies are developing an allergy to cow's milk. These allergens can be from foodstuffs we eat or drink, things we inhale, are injected with or other substances that we come in contact with. The list of allergens is extensive as are the symptoms they can produce, so I will only be able to deal with the most common allergies.

Tips on allergies

* Allergies are an **inherited** trait (to lessen the chance see **Pre-conceptual Care**). Your child is more likely to develop an allergy if either parent has an allergy. If both parents have allergies, this multiplies the chances considerably.

* The allergy inherited is not necessarily the one either parent may have already. For example the mother may have asthma and the child may get eczema.

* If there are allergies in your family history it would be better to **breastfeed** your baby if it is possible.

* If there is a high risk of allergy it may be worth avoiding possible offending substances for the first year of life. For example you could avoid milk and milk products, wheat, eggs and artificial colourants and preservatives.

* When weaning or introducing these substances to the diet go carefully and wait forty eight hours to watch for any reaction.

* **Smoking** aggravates a lot of these allergic conditions - don't allow smoking in your house.

* **Signs and symptoms** that may lead you to suspect your child has an allergy are: constant coughs and wheezes; runny nose; excess mucus; ear problems (glue ear); sensitive skin; eczema; hives; frequent nappy rash; skin quickly becoming sore around mouth or nose if the child has a cold; migraine; headaches; hyperactivity; tension/fatigue syndrome (ie appearing pale or run down with black rings under their eyes). It can affect the digestive system in various ways, for example repeated mouth ulcers; tummy pains; colic or anal soreness. Other general symptoms may be bedwetting or aching joints.

* **Common allergens** are:

  Foodstuffs: cow's milk and milk products, eggs, citrus fruits, chocolate, cheese, wheat, fish, peanuts, tomatoes, mushrooms, artificial colourants and preservatives.

  Additives: E102-155 (AZO and Coal tar dye), E210-230 (Preservative), E310-321 (Antioxidants).

  Inhaled allergens: house dust, feathers, animal fur, pollens.

* Foods least likely to cause allergic reactions are lamb, polished rice, carrots, lettuce, peeled potatoes, pears, sunflower oil.

What to do   * Keep a strict record of everything your child eats and drinks over a period of one week, plus any symptoms that occur. This could help pinpoint an **allergen**.

* Get yourself a sympathetic GP and show her/him all the records you have made, then work together as a team to identify the allergen. This may be more difficult than it seems, as sometimes it can be a combination of substances.

* Your doctor may order **allergy testing**. This usually consists of the skin-pricking test. This involves placing drops of the substances thought to be causing the allergic reaction on the child's skin. If a reaction occurs it is a positive result and the child is allergic to the substance. Sometimes blood tests may be taken in order to observe a reaction to particular foods.

* Avoid contact with the allergen once it is identified. For example, if the child is allergic to fur, no pets should be allowed in the house.

* If we are unable to avoid it entirely we may be able to take steps to limit contact. For example, allergy to **dust** means the house must be vacuumed and dusted regularly. Use synthetic bedding material, cover mattress with a plastic sheet. Don't leave clothes lying around to collect dust.

* If the child is allergic to **pollen**, decisions must be taken as to the best treatment, be it medication or desensitisation. Avoid parks and fields on high pollen count days and keep the car window shut when travelling.

* **Foods** that are identified as causing reactions should be eliminated from the diet. Again this is easier said than done sometimes. It can be just a part of the food that causes problems. For example, it may be just the egg white and the reaction might not occur if the egg is thoroughly boiled.

* Sometimes the child can tolerate the allergen in different forms. For example the small amount of egg in cakes may not cause a reaction.

* With your doctor's supervision an **avoidance diet** may be agreed upon. For example, a milk-free diet could help for excess mucus, eczema, asthma. A milk/egg, artificial colourant and preservative-free diet may help relieve eczema and hyperactivity.

* Treatment of allergies usually involves a lot of parental controlling and involvement. It can be a terrible hassle and mean lots of extra work for the parents involved. But the good news is most allergies do improve with age. Gradually you may be able to re-introduce all the foods back into the diet as time goes on. (see **Food Hints**).

Hyperactivity

The name hyperactive is given to children with many and varied symptoms, these include: the inability to concentrate on one thing, losing interest quickly, attention switching quickly from one thing to another, unceasing restlessness and over activity. There may be behaviourial problems which affect relationships with others, or the child may be disruptive at school and frequently disobedient. About 50% of hyperactive children appear to be poor learners but that may be because they can't concentrate or sit still long enough to remember or apply all the information they are given. The child may appear immature and continue to 'baby talk' longer than peers. These children often are poor sleepers and have a poor appetite, causing added concern to already upset parents. Parents may even describe their child as having an 'unhappy' disposition. There may also be physical symptoms such as headaches, tummy pains, diarrhoea, runny nose, eczema, hay fever, and/or intense thirst. Of course just because your child has one or indeed a couple of these symptoms does not mean she is hyperactive. You and your doctor need to assess all the behaviourial and physical symptoms carefully before jumping to that conclusion.

It was in the 1970s that a Dr Feingold first suggested that certain foods and artificial colourants and preservatives may be causing hyperactivity. It is still not fully proven that he is correct although I know many parents who agree with him. Any parent who has watched how their own child behaves after going to a party where they were given lots of so-called goodies, will have no doubt as to the logic of his theory. So if you basically agree that there is or may be a link between diet and the behaviour problems of hyperactivity read on. Finally I often think the parents of hyperactive children need as much care and attention as the child; it is a very demanding task to take care of these children. So throughout it all parents must not forget their own needs too. Take time to yourself to relax and do the things that give you pleasure. Get babysitters so that you can continue your leisure activities. This will help you have the extra patience needed for the trials of coping with your hyperactive child. Treating the problem nutritionally may bring about such a change in your child that you may come to realise (as I have) that the saying 'we are what we eat' is really true and you may then want to change the whole family's diet to a more wholesome, additive-free one.

Tips * The first step to take is to write down point by point what **behaviour problems** your child has. Then list any **physical symptoms**. If you have a list of approximately five to ten points that tally with the symptoms I have already mentioned it is worth taking your child (and your list) to your GP for assessment.

* The idea behind the treatment is to eliminate all **processed foods**, especially those which contain certain additives that have been found to produce certain sensitive or adverse reactions in other children.

* Nutritional treatment of hyperactivity encourages a natural, more **wholesome diet**. In other words junk food out, fresh home cooking in and no snacks in between meals.

* If however instead of behaviour problems, your child's symptoms are more physical ones such as eczema, colic, runny nose, sleeplessness, constant nappy rash, the doctor may suspect that your child may have a sensitivity to milk or other foodstuffs. Therefore a diet eliminating the foodstuffs or milk products may be prescribed.

* Your doctor may need to do **allergy testing** to check that his diagnosis to what your child may be sensitive to is correct.

* Some doctors also prescribe **Evening Primrose Oil**, especially if, following the partial success of the elimination diet, intense thirst continues as a symptom.

* In my experience some doctors are more aware and sensitive to the treatment of the hyperactive child than others. So do get yourself a sympathetic GP or an allergy specialist or paediatrician who is used to dealing with this disorder.

* Join your national HYPERACTIVE CHILDREN'S SUPPORT GROUP who not only give support to parents but lots of useful information too (see the back of this book for addresses).

* Look closely at the **labels** on the food you buy. The label should have a list of what is contained in the product. Look carefully to see that any of the additives known to cause reactions are not added (see list). But better still go for fresh food. Remember too that the label may just state permitted colourants, in which case you cannot be sure which of the additives it contains.

* It is best to try if you can to eliminate all processed food from your child's diet, but particularly the following:

  E102 (Tartrazine Yellow), E104 (Quinoline Yellow), E107 (Yellow 2Q), E110 (Sunset Yellow), E122 (Carmoisine - red), E123 (Amaranth - red), E124 (Ponceau 4R - red), E127 (Erythrosine), E131-133 (blues), E150 (Caramel), E151 (Black PN), E154 (Brown FK), E155 (Chocolate Brown HT). These are found in food containing fat such as desserts, sweets, juices, soups, sauces, vegetables. Adverse reactions may include, hyperactivity, eczema, wheezing, wakefulness

E210-E219 and Benzoic Acid are found in jam, juices, desserts, preservatives, tinned fruit, and yoghurt, and may cause skin rashes.

Others to watch out for are: E250 (Sodium Nitrate), found in cooked meats; E251; E320 (Butylated hydrozyanisole, BHA), used in fats; E321 (hydroxytoluene, BHT); E621 (Monosodium glutamate, MSG); E622 (Monopotassium glutamate); and E623 (Calcium glutamate).

There are many more. For an up-to-date list contact your local support group.

* Try to eliminate or at least cut down on **salicyclates**. These are found in dried fruits, oranges, berry fruits, pineapples, cucumbers, tomato sauce. They are also found in medicines containing aspirin so watch out for those. Use paracetamol-based ones instead. Please note: you should never give aspirin to young children.

* Food that may commonly contain these **colourants** and **preservatives** are: coloured sweets, puddings, cordial, squashes, fizzy drinks, jam, ice lollies, lollipops, ice cream, yoghurt, chocolate sweets, manufactured sauces, salad creams, cakes, biscuits, soups, custard.

* It is very important here to emphasise that only between 1% and 2% of children appear to be really sensitive to these substances. So it is important to keep hyperactivity in the right perspective.

* Parents of a hyperactive child can become exhausted and emotionally overwrought. To be told to put the child on a **special diet** may seem to be an extra pressure. But please do give the diet a chance. It will be hard at first as children tend to love and really want the food that is actually causing the problems, but stick with it. I have seen so-called disruptive, unhappy children transformed into happy, healthy children again after having their diet changed in this way.

Ear and eye problems

The most common ear problem in the pre-school child is earache and from this the condition commonly called 'glue ear' can occur.

The most common eye problems that occur in the child under sixteen years of age are visual difficulties and squints (eye muscle difficulties). I will be dealing with these problems in the following pages.

The ear

In the very young child ear problems are extremely common and it is important we understand how the ear works so we can watch out for any problems. Hearing difficulties can delay progress in speech and communication if not picked up in the early stages.

How to recognise ear problems

* The ear is divided into three parts - the outer, middle and inner ear. The outer ear consists of the canal. The middle ear contains the eardrum and the inner ear contains an organ which is filled with fluid. The outer ear collects sound waves, the ear drum vibrates and these vibrations are passed into the inner ear, where they are changed to nerve impulses which go to the brain and allow us to hear.

* You can suspect an ear problem if your infant has a cold, wakes up at night and seems to be in pain and is constantly pulling or touching the ears.

* An earache can occur after recurrent sore throats or colds, followed by ear infections.

* Severe earache, heavy discharge from the ear, fever or vomiting are not normal so if any of these occur see your doctor immediately as they could indicate infection.

* Paracetamol can be given to soothe, and a course of antibiotics may be prescribed.

* Raise the head of the cot/bed slightly to aid drainage of the fluid from the ear, to prevent night time earache and waking.

* Avoid getting the infant chilled in the winter and avoid people with colds. Give cod liver oil and extra Vitamin C where possible, especially in winter time.

* The 'glue ear' occurs because in the very young infant the eustachian tube (the tube leading from the throat to the ear) is very short and infections from the throat and bad colds can easily travel up to the middle ear where the eardrum is situated. The ear can then become infected and eventually fills with sticky fluid instead of air. This then prevents the natural travel of sound and can affect the infant's hearing.

* This hearing difficulty can then hinder the child's speech, for it is around this time that a child's speech development is at its greatest. If you think your child's speech is not progressing as well as it should do it may be a good idea to have a hearing test done.

* If the doctor suspects any hearing difficulties s/he may order an audiogram which tests the hearing more accurately.

* If a 'glue ear' is diagnosed, grommets may be inserted into the child's ear. Grommets are small plastic or metal tubes which are placed inside the ear to allow the drainage of the sticky fluid that has collected in the ear, thus allowing the sound to pass through unhindered. These are put in place under general anaesthetic by an ear, nose and throat specialist in hospital. The fluid is first sucked out and the grommet is left in place to drain any further fluid, usually for about a year, although the time varies from child to child. The child generally stays in hospital overnight but is fine again in about a week.

* Be very careful whilst washing your child's hair, or going swimming as no water should enter the ear. Your doctor might advise you to use earplugs, or a simple ball of cotton wool may be used when washing hair.

* A grommet may work its way out of the ear, so watch out for this.

* If your infant is prone to earache and 'glue ear', cut down on dairy products, as they encourage the production of secretions.

* This condition can be very distressing for the child as anyone who has suffered with earache knows, so plenty of nutritious fluids and tender loving care are needed.

The eye

The eye is like a strong balloon, spherical in shape, situated in a bony cavity of the skull. The wall of the eye consists of three layers. The outer one (the sclera) continues forward and becomes the cornea, the transparent window of the eye we see through. The middle wall is the choroid and this becomes the muscle that holds and controls the lens and the iris (the coloured part) of the eye. In the centre there is a hole called the pupil. The retina, the inner wall, holds the light-sensitive cells which pass the messages to the optic or seeing nerve. We need the cornea and pupil to bend and control the amount of light entering the eye (for example in bright light we constrict the pupil). It is also important for the rays of light entering the eye to do so at the same point in both eyes to stimulate the same part of the retina (the seeing part) simultaneously. Movements of the eyeball and equal muscle control of both eyes are important, otherwise double vision can occur. The eye is like a sensitive camera. Light rays are focused on the retina, producing an image and any obstruction or focusing difficulty can produce fuzzy images. If sight difficulties occur in the baby or young child the eye may just stop functioning and sight may be lost, so it very important to detect any eye problems at the earliest time possible to stop this from happening.

Eye problems	Focusing problems: There are generally three types of focusing difficulties, short sightedness (myopia): distant objects cannot be seen clearly. Long sightedness (hypermetropia): difficulty in seeing both very near and distant objects. This is common in childhood, and can cause the child to squint. Astigmatism: the cornea (the transparent window in front of the pupil and iris) is not curved smoothly and may bend the light rays in the wrong direction.

* These conditions need treatment or the eyes may squint in order to try to correct the visual difficulties they are having. If a squinting eye is not treated it will then cause double vision. The brain cannot cope with this, so it literally shuts down the sight of the eye with the defect. If left untreated the eye will eventually stop seeing. That is why to preserve sight in the eye it is of the utmost importance to report any eye squints or even slight turns to your doctor immediately so treatment can commence.

* The newborn baby has to learn to accommodate near and far objects so very young babies can occasionally be unsteady with their eye movements, but if your baby consistently moves one eye out of turn with the other do not hesitate to check it out with your doctor. The sooner these defects are treated the better the chance of normal vision in both eyes.

* If your child has been diagnosed as having a visual defect it is of the utmost importance to carry out the treatment prescribed by the eye specialist - this usually consists of wearing glasses.

* If the doctor instructs the child to wear the glasses all the time, make sure s/he does.

* Children wearing glasses for the first time should be treated with tender care. Explain the importance of wearing the glasses and choose a pair which the child likes. Practise role playing so that the child will know how to cope with any teasing that occurs. Point out famous people or favourite uncles and aunts who wear glasses.

* Generally squints may be noticed for the first time when the child is tired or sick.

* If the vision of the squinting eye has already got 'lazy' or deteriorated the doctor may order a patch for the good eye to encourage the squinting eye to work harder. Again if this treatment is ordered it is vitally important you ensure it is done, for once the child reaches the age of eight the vision can be lost for good.

* Patching the 'good' eye may be the only way of getting the faulty eye to see properly again. But the patching may need to be done in stages, for as you can imagine it could be dangerous for a child not to see properly. So it may be ordered only for certain times during the day at first, gradually leading to continuous patching as the weak eye improves.

* However long the patching lasts be very careful with your child, watch out for little accidents and be sympathetic if they occur. Be especially careful on the roads.

* Always have a positive attitude to the glasses. Praise the child for keeping them on, keep them clean and treat the glasses with respect, being careful to not put them 'lens down' when not in use to avoid scratches. Buy an attractive glasses case to keep them in.

* A specialist may need to check the vision of your child and assess the amount of squint that is present and may also order special exercises to be done. Again, as with all the treatments prescribed, make sure they are done, to preserve your child's vision.

* Eye surgery can be performed to correct the squinting eye. This makes the eye look cosmetically good but does not generally correct the vision. So the treatment of wearing glasses and patching may need to be continued.

* Eye surgery consists of adjusting the outer eye muscles so they pull the eyeball into the correct position, by extending the muscle on one side and tightening it on the other. This can be performed on a day-patient basis or it may necessitate an overnight stay in hospital. The eye is generally red and sore for a couple of days afterwards. Giving Paracetamol to soothe and keeping the lights dimmed helps.

* A squint (medical name: strabismus) is common and occurs in approximately three out of every hundred children, so be on the look-out for it and get treatment as soon as possible. Suspect it if your child's eyes are not straight when looking at any object, or seem not to be in line together; the other eye may turn inwards or outwards and occasionally upwards.

* Children of the child's own age may not notice the turning eye but older children may notice and can be cruel. Don't just dismiss this. Teach the child how to cope with teasing as it may damage confidence if you don't. Always be positive and supportive and you could turn a difficulty into a positive experience.

Vomiting

Vomiting occurs when the stomach empties its contents quickly. The child may complain of feeling sick or being nauseated beforehand. Others may complain of a pain in their stomach, or babies who have no way of communicating may just vomit without warning. Vomiting is one of the body's defense mechanisms against infection, against too much food, unwanted food they may be sensitive to, or even food that may be poisonous. A child may be sick because s/he is overexcited, at the onset of an illness, when s/he has a bout of coughing or if s/he is under stress. It may cause the stomach muscles to be tight, not allowing food to be properly digested. Vomiting is a symptom of many different illnesses and has a variety of causes, but most of the reasons for vomiting are not serious. As a general rule, if your child is suddenly sick but feels and looks well afterwards, there is no need for concern.

Tips on coping with vomiting

* A baby vomiting a small amount of milk - say, a few teaspoons full - just after a feed, is normal. It is called possetting. If your baby is prone to this happening be careful to wind regularly and keep upright after the feed. Remember to keep a protective nappy or towel handy at all times for you shoulder or your lap, otherwise your clothes will get ruined. Don't move the baby about too much after the feed.

* If a breast-fed baby vomits the mother should revise her diet - over-spiced foods, very fatty foods, too much tea, coffee or alcohol may not agree with the baby.

* If the vomiting happens regularly in small amounts as you feed or wind, check that the hole in the teat is the correct size and the baby is not swallowing too much air if the hole is too small, or cannot cope with the excess milk if the hole is too big.

* If you see bits of undigested food in the vomited matter, or if s/he is stressed or over-excited, sit and gently soothe the child.

* If the child has a cold and swallows the mucus, you will see the mucus in the vomit. Blow the child's nose on a regular basis to prevent this, or teach the child how to do this, blowing one nostril at a time.

* If you think your child may have swallowed something that is causing the vomiting, call your GP for advice.

* Sometimes children use vomiting to manipulate parents. In these cases stay calm, be supportive and kind but firm, wipe up the sick and it's off to school or back to bed. If it does not get them what they want they will stop doing it.

* Some babies/children are more prone to being sick than others - all you can do is be prepared with a sick bag, change of clothes, and towels to protect you.

* While a child is being sick be supportive, calm and reassuring. Place a cool damp cloth on the forehead and hold the child as s/he is sick into a bucket (or whatever is handy). The mouth should be swilled out afterwards. The child may need to sleep after the effort of vomiting. Place a bucket or bowl nearby in case of emergencies.

* Most cases of vomiting are not serious but if you are unsure and there are any other signs of illness or if the symptoms mentioned below are present, call a doctor.

**When to call
your doctor**

* A newborn baby (under three months old) vomits with a lot of force, causing projectile vomiting. This could be pyloric stenosis, when the opening of the stomach is too tight. It needs an operation to correct it, which is highly successful.

* A baby vomits a couple of times in one hour, or after each feed, and nappies remain dry. Also if there is no obvious reason for the vomiting.

* The vomiting follows a head injury or a fall of some kind.

* The baby has diarrhoea as well as vomiting and is under two years of age.

* The child vomits and has obvious abdominal pain, intermittently or continuously.

* The vomited matter contains blood, and/or the stools passed contain blood or mucus.

* Vomiting occurs with pain around tummy button and to the lower right side. This could indicate appendicitis.

* Vomiting and bed wetting occur with pain below tummy button, back and front. This could be a urinary tract infection, especially prevalent in little girls.

* Extreme drowsiness is combined with the vomiting.

* A high temperature is present with the vomiting and after tepid sponging it does not settle down. This may be the start of another illness.

Give a child who has vomited sips of cool water or ice to suck, but if after twelve hours s/he cannot tolerate clear fluids, seek advice. Of course do not offer a sick child food, but give plenty of water and fluids when s/he can take them, to replace fluid loss. If diarrhoea is present with the vomiting treat as for diarrhoea.

Things to do

I cannot emphasise enough the importance of children's play - that does not mean parents have to go out and buy loads of toys, half of which may fall apart on the first day. But it does mean that we as parents may need to exercise our imagination and point the young ones in the right direction. Also watch out for, collect and save items that may be used as play things. Do remember that sometimes the cardboard boxes some fancy toys come in, are played with more than the actual games themselves. In picking games or activities for 'things to do' I have chosen cheap, easy things that will stretch the child's imagination. Some of them that seem simple to us, children adore doing - remember that fantasy and magic are all part of our children's wonderful world. In this highly technological world let's not deny our children the sort of play that dreams are made of. When buying any toys, always check for sturdiness, little things that may break off, and think of time/value - how long will your child be interested in it? A lot of the pretend toys such as cookers, sandpits, dolls houses and robots can all be made out of cardboard boxes, or odds and ends lying around the house - make them together, the children may enjoy them more. Some bought toys are necessary but just try them out on the made-up one first to make sure they really want it. You can never have enough crayons, paints, paper and glue - buy in bulk and save yourself time and effort. I have concentrated on the younger child because as children grow older they tend to lean less on parents to help them; they just make their own fun. But you may find that some of the games adapt well for older children too.

Indoors   *   Encourage **self-sufficiency** in your children. Let them help you in any task they enjoy doing. When washing up give them a bowl with lots of suds in, let them wash all the spoons. Say thank you and they'll grow in confidence.

  *   **Books** are a must in every household; encourage the love of them. You can make your own with pictures cut from magazines or newspapers, stick them onto paper or just thread them together with a piece of string. Write a word naming the object in the picture at the bottom. You could let them make a *Book about myself*: write their name (or let them do it) and let them draw themselves or stick in a photo and let them reveal themselves on every page, one page for my friends, my holidays, my favourite things, and so on. Even older children love doing this.

* Make your own **jigsaw**. Let your children pick a big picture they especially like, paste it to a piece of card or cardboard, leave to dry then cut up into easy sections. As your children get older you can let the jigsaw become more complicated. Make a huge jigsaw for bringing into the garden on sunny days.

* All children are artists: have lots of **crayons**, the large non-toxic type at first. Pin old wall paper on to the wall at drawing level and let them at it.

* **Modelling games** are another great treat - always have a supply of glue handy (the ones with a big washable brush are the best buy). Collect egg boxes, tin foil, bottle tops, toilet rolls, kitchen rolls, cereal packets, yoghurt pots, ice cream containers. Make space ships, castles, trains, trucks. Always ask for your shoe box at the shoe shop - it makes a great bed, train trailer, puppet theatre, jewellery box, and so on.

* **Collage** is wonderful for most ages. Have a collage box with cotton wool, old pieces of material, gold lame, velvet, sequins. Or have a kitchen collage made with pasta shapes, rice, lentils, herbs, beans of all colours and shapes. Or have a garden collage, using leaves and flowers in your garden, let the children stick them all on paper and make pictures and see what emerges.

* **Sorting games** can be played with stones, pasta, beans, or buttons. Put them all together and put out pots for the child to sort them into.

* **Matching games**: choose a theme like 'colour' and pick all the black things in a magazine, then all the red things and so on. Have one page for each colour, stick pictures of one colour on to one page, print the name of the colour clearly at the top. Gradually widen the game to include the names of things and spellings.

* **Guessing games**: put an object in a paper bag and let the child feel it and guess what it is.

* **Memory games**: put a few objects on to a tray. The child looks at the tray for a minute, then you take one object away and s/he guesses which one is gone. Or you could make the child close their eyes and name all the things on the tray. Add more objects for the older child.

* **Funny people**: the first player draws a funny face on a piece of paper, folds the paper over, and passes it on to the next person, who draws a body, the next draws the legs and so on. At the end, the funny person is revealed.

* Make the most of **music**: use a wooden spoon with a pan, and rice in a pot, or provide real instruments such as tambourines or recorders.

* Encourage them to learn **rhymes and songs**. Get a tape recorder, let them hear themselves, keep the tape so you can remember every stage yourself. Start with them just clapping out the notes, and work towards them playing the notes on the recorder. Remember there is nothing like a good old sing-song.

* Play classical as well as pop music, let them mime out **playing an instrument** like the violin and the trumpet - it's great fun.

* Always keep any old fancy clothes in a **dressing-up** box for children. In fact, sometimes it is the accessories that are more important than the clothes; go to the local jumble sale or keep your eyes open as you go around for handbags, worker's hard hats, police helmets, caps, straw hats - you name it. Cloaks can be made from old curtains, or tablecloths, gloves, scarves, belts. Don't forget to keep feathers for an Indian head dress, old spectacles without lenses, old jewellery. These and many more can be great for disguises, or making up characters for a play.

* Make **play dough**. Mix four tablespoons of cream of tartar, two cups of plain flour, one cup of salt, then add two cups of water, food colouring and two tablespoons of oil. Cook over a low heat for three to five minutes, stirring well. The play dough will last for ages kept in a lidded container. Use a rolling pin and cutters of all shapes and have hours of fun.

* Do **cook** with children from an early age, even if they only sift the flour or put out the paper cups for fairy cakes at first. Gradually they'll improve and become little cooks in their own right.

* **Printing** of all sorts is fun - use a potato cut into different shapes and make hand prints, footprints, leaf prints, string prints. Paper doilies also make pretty prints.

* Playing at **shop** is easy to arrange. Keep cereal packets, tape them closed, keep any loose goods like beans and vegetables, supply a few paper bags, and a big scoop.

* Make **puppets** from spoons, socks, gloves, paper bags, or just from a picture in a magazine stuck on a straw. A decorated box can be a great puppet theatre from behind the couch.

* I hope you have had your imagination tickled by now and

can think of lots more ideas to keep your children happy and occupied.

Outdoors * You will need shallow dishes, egg-boxes, jam-jars, seed trays and flower pots.

* Let the children grow things for themselves. Start off with **mustard and cress** seeds made out in their initials - put the seeds into some cotton wool in an egg box, keep the wool moist and watch them grow together.

* Cut the tops off carrots, parsnip, beetroot, or any root vegetable, place in a saucer of water and watch them grow.

* Plant **bulbs** like daffodil, tulip, hyacinth, or cuttings from a spider plant.

* Buy a packet of **seeds** that give reliable results: nasturtium, beans, sweet peas, marigold, forget-me-not's.

* Sprout **beans** such as mung, aduki, alfalfa. Simply place the beans on a piece of moist cotton wool.

* Grow **flowers** for drying. You can use packets of Honesty, straw daisy, or poppy seeds. These can be dried out and painted silver, gold or pretty colours.

* Grow **plants** from stones. An avocado stone should be soaked for two days first, then put in a glass jar almost full of water, the large end just touching the water. Use cocktail sticks to balance. After two weeks the stone will split and a root will appear. Date stones can be planted straight into damp compost. Plant three to four of the stones in a pot in a clear plastic bag, tie the top tightly and leave in a warm, dark place keeping the compost moist. They will sprout in three to four weeks. Peach and plum stones should be squeezed slightly with a nut cracker first, then planted like the date.

* A **herb garden** is an achievement which the children can actually eat. Grow parsley from seeds, rosemary from a cutting taken in September, chives from a clump of the plant. Mint can also be grown from a clump, but it can go wild so watch it.

* Give each child their own **patch of garden** and encourage them to be responsible for weeding and watering and planting. Mark out their own patch with stones, wood, shells, or whatever comes naturally in or around your garden. Paint their names on a stone or poster covered in plastic, for example, *Pat's Patch*.

* Do make a point of having a **bird area** with bird cake, a string of peanuts or scraps.

* Observe **nature**, watching and talking about the beauty of the seasons as they occur.

* Don't forget the pleasure of making **daisy chains**.

* Collect **fir cones** and paint them for Christmas.

* If you have any little cracks in the pavement around your house, fill them in with alyssum seeds in March.

* Have a **nature trail** in the garden, finding snails, caterpillars, ladybirds - talk about the beauty of each living creature and what they do.

* Drawing leaves and plants in the open air is a great pastime. You could also try bark rubbing or leaf tracing.

* **Collect seeds** from other people's gardens or your own. Try wallflower, sunflower, lupin seeds - keep them in an envelope in a cool, dry place until the spring comes, then plant them. Don't forget to label them so you know what you are sowing.

* Keep a diary recording the progress of the developing plants. Get a **gardening** book, prepare the children for biology at school.

* The rule of gardening is always to give your hands a good wash afterwards.

* Teach your children to recognise poisonous plants, seeds, flowers and leaves from an early age.

* **Garden dens** are a little hideaway for many adventures - encourage or help your children build one.

* Remember **picnics** in the garden are always a pleasure - it's great to eat outdoors when we can and it gives children a keen appetite.

* Outdoor **treasure hunts** are great fun.

* Encourage them to care for the natural **environment** and teach children to care for the world in which we live. They can read about nature from books at the local library. Join EARTHWATCH or the equivalent in your country (addresses at the back of this book).

* Country **walks** or walking to school sometimes (if possible) can lead to wonderful moments shared together.

* Encourage **outdoor activities** such as rounders, football, hockey, tennis. Get them interested in sport from a early age to keep them fit and healthy. Make the most of the great outdoors.

* Other outdoor games:

   Simon says: touch your nose, jump up and down, clap your hands, etc,

   Fill the bucket: two teams line up with an empty bucket for the leader and at the other end of the garden, a full bucket of water is waiting - you get the idea. The winning team is the one who has the most water in their bucket at the end.

   Wheel barrow races: These are lots of fun.

   What's the time Mr Wolf?: all the children follow Mr Wolf and ask what's the time and when it's dinner time he runs after them unless they escape to 'den'.

   Sleeping Lions: everyone needs to stay still, for when the lion sees you move he can wake up and catch you for dinner.

   Musical statues: can be played outside with someone singing, or an open air disco is a great idea.

* If you get the chance for your child to do horse riding, sailing or any type of water sports or outside activities like camping, jump at the chance.

Parenting
survival strategies

Special survival strategies for mother

* Advertisements constantly pressurise women with stereotypical images of how a mother should behave. There is no one, ideal way of mothering your children - all mothers are unique, and rightly so.

* The responsibilities of motherhood are **learnt**; have a few good books for looking up specific help, but talking to friends and family who have 'been there' is very helpful and comforting.

* Encourage all the people you know to **participate** in your parenting role, encourage them to make relationships with your children.

* Get to know other people who are experienced in child rearing - learn from them.

* Get your **priorities** right. Do not overload yourself with unimportant tasks. Make a list of things to do today if necessary.

* Try not to be concerned with keeping up **appearances**. Be honest with yourself and others. If you cannot cope, say so.

* Look after Number One, (that's you). **Time to yourself** is essential. Your health and well-being is essential for your baby's care too.

* **Exercise** every day and get some fresh air and sunshine if there is any about. When you are away from your baby enjoy yourself. Enjoy being yourself for a while.

* It is essential to get a good **support system** going, through family, friends, neighbours. Or organise a babysitting circle if there are a few of you in the same position. Advertise in the local shop window if you must but get a regular babysitter you can trust.

* Join a **group** to meet other mothers, be it a mother and toddler group, a church group, a local play group, the NATIONAL CHILDBIRTH TRUST (addresses at the back of this book). Find out what is going on locally and join. If you're a mother who works outside the home as well, a support system is essential, preferably with a back-up in case of emergencies.

* Most mothers I know are anxious to get their figures back after having a baby. But dieting at this time is a bad idea - it makes most of us grumpy. Instead be careful to eat a sensible **wholefood diet** containing lots of fresh produce. Eat in moderation and take plenty of exercise and your body will eventually return to its pre-pregnancy weight.

* **Relaxation** of some sort is a must for all mothers. Take time for this purpose, don't feel guilty about it or wonder about the things you could be doing. There are many ways of relaxing, sleep is one, relaxing in a warm bath is another. Using the breathing techniques taught in antenatal class can be another way. You could try Transcendental Meditation, yoga or swimming. Remember motherhood is only a part of you. Keep up your interests and continue to see your friends.

* Motherhood is a learnt skill so we are continuously learning. There are no real set rules except be kind to yourself, relax and enjoy your children.

Special survival strategies for father

* Your partner will need **extra care** during pregnancy, especially for the first three months. Give her breakfast in bed, a lie-in or just an hour or two's rest from the children. Do the shopping and as much housework as possible.

* Talk to the baby in the womb - it'll make you feel daft at first, but it's only the start of your second childhood as well as your baby's first.

* **Attending the birth** of your baby is the most extraordinary experience - don't miss it! Even for the second and the third, experience doesn't teach you everything, but for the first, be prepared to be 'blown away'. No books (even this one!) can do any more than hint at the power of the event - it's as if your whole life has been compressed and explodes into a staggering new creation. I'd give any odds that you cry!

* **Change the first nappy!** Don't let anyone tell you the messy stuff is fun for the first few times, but you do get used to it.

* Take as much time off work as you can from the time the baby is due home. It's such a pleasure to share the first few days. But don't forget that sometimes the troubles can come when it seems both of you have settled into a routine - any time in the first year the bubble can burst. Relentless crying, vomiting, red-raw bums - it's important to share in these agonies so that both deep down understand what it is like to want to throw away the baby you swore you'd love for every minute of eternity. It is only then you recognise the difficulty as well as the joy of bringing up your child. If the difficulties become too great (and depression can affect men as well as women) get help from family, friends, doctor, or those listed at the back of this book.

* After the birth, do as much as you can as a family unit, shopping, walks, meals, baths, swimming etc. It will bring you all closer together.

* Spend time alone with your baby, playing games, reading, just cuddling. The simple happenings will give you memories for a life time.

* Take the pressure off your partner by doing your share of the jobs without having to be asked or asking about them. Explaining jobs is as dreary as doing them.

* Give yourself time by cutting down on the TV and newspapers - what you learn and remember from them is nothing compared to what children will give you.

* If and when you're sure your family is complete, think seriously about a **vasectomy** (male sterilisation). With the woman still carrying the bulk of the family burden it is only fair that you do your bit.

* **Love them** - it's that simple.

Minimising stress and worry

Everyone worries too much at times, especially parents with so much to do and remember. You may even be feeling the signs of too much stress in your life already, so what can you do about it? Here are a few hints to help.

Tips

* As soon as you have started a family, review your life insurance cover and make a will.

* **Talk about your problems.** A problem shared is a problem halved.

* **Write it out.** List all your options and what you need to do. Writing it down may put it in the right perspective. Weigh up the pros and cons, make a decision, and then act on it.

* Try **delaying tactics**: if you really need time to think about something, put aside fifteen minutes for a 'worry session' and leave it until then.

* **Exercise** will clear your head and divert energies. Instead of bottling up tension, channel your emotions into something constructive, walk, jog, do gardening, shadow box if you must Work it off!

* **Explore alternatives.** Consider taking the opposite approach to the obvious one: what really would happen?

* **Laugh it off.** My mother always says, 'A smile costs nothing'. Lighten your troubles and be generous with smiles: they tend to return to you.

* **Think positively:** don't let the negative side pull you down, but consider the good consequences and feel glad about them. Then picture the worst: could it really happen and is it likely?

* **Give way occasionally.** Children can be obstinate and defiant sometimes. Go easy on yourself and others at times. You are only a human being. You'll be relieved from the pressure of 'having to do things right' all of the time.

* Try not to be too critical of yourself and others. **Concentrate on your good points**, you'll feel less let down by yourself and others.

* **Don't compete** with others. The other person's grass is not greener, even though sometimes it may look that way. The perfect parent does not exist - we all have our own particular problems to cope with. Don't upset yourself by reaching for goals we cannot attain.

* Take **one step at a time**. Select the most urgent tasks and do them one by one. Tension can make an ordinary day overwhelming. Make a list of what you have to do and leave the rest. Don't try to be a perfectionist. This is an open invitation to fail. Be easy on yourself.

* **Imagine success.** Day-dream about the best outcome.

* Plan your **recreation** time. No matter how short it is, don't waste it. Use it well and you'll see problems in a new, refreshing, different light. Even if it is only a short time, take time off for yourself every day. If possible get a day away from the family, or a long weekend. A holiday away would really rest you and make you appreciate them a little more too.

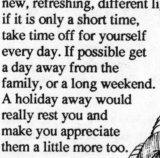

* **Relax.** Learn and practise exercise and methods of relaxation every day. This will help you unlock tension in every part of your body, and prevents anxiety and therefore future stress-related illnesses.

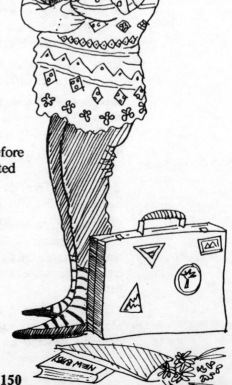

Contraception

From my experience as a woman, mother and parent, contraception is not far from the mind of every parent. A fertile woman has an opportunity to conceive nearly every month and for health and economic reasons, not to mention social and emotional concerns, having pregnancy after pregnancy is not acceptable for most couples. With the contraception methods available now it should be possible for a couple to have sex whenever they want to without the fear of an unwanted pregnancy. This gives parents the freedom to plan their families to suit their own needs. It is also worth mentioning that the unplanned pregnancy rate is very high in the first few months after childbirth - forewarned is forearmed (I hope). Here is a brief outline of the methods that are available at the moment.

'Natural' methods

These methods really rely on the woman observing her body changes and knowing when she is fertile and refraining from having sex at the fertile time in her cycle (or using a barrier method at the fertile time). There are associations throughout the country that specialise in teaching this method (see the back of this book for addresses).

Billings ovulation or mucus method	These methods are based on observing the woman's cervical mucus discharge. The discharge varies throughout each month and at the fertile phase the mucus gets very thick, sticky and stringy, and if you put it between your finger and thumb, feels a bit like soft chewing gum.
The temperature method	The basal body temperature rises slightly when an egg is released. So by taking a daily temperature reading and making out a graph we can gauge when a woman is likely to be fertile.
Sympto-thermal method (Rhythm method)	The sympto-thermal method combines the mucus and temperature method. All of these 'natural' methods can be successful, but the couple needs to be extremely well motivated, and the success rate depends entirely on the correct assessment of the woman's bodily changes, which can be affected by illness, stress or emotion. Human error is also an important factor.

151

The withdrawal method	To my mind this is not a reliable form of contraception, but needs to be mentioned as it is still used by some couples. The man simply withdraws his penis from the vagina before he ejaculates. It relies on the man knowing exactly when he is about to come and requires great self-control. This method carries a high risk of pregnancy, not only because of the will involved but because the lubricating fluid secreted prior to the 'come' also contains some sperm. Please do not rely on it as your only form of contraception if you really do not want to get pregnant.
Breast-feeding	Breastfeeding on demand can prevent you ovulating (making an egg) but you need to be breastfeeding every two to three hours without a long break at night and missing no feeds for it to be really effective. Once you miss feeds or the baby sleeps for long periods at night, or you start weaning, breastfeeding may no longer prevent an egg from being produced so you may be capable of becoming pregnant.

Male methods

The condom (sheath / french letter)	The condom is made of thin rubber and should be rolled over the erect penis prior to sexual contact. It then acts as a container for the semen when the man ejaculates from his penis as he 'comes'. A spermicide should be used with this method. The success rate again varies depending on how carefully the method is used, but the failure rate can be as low as 4% or as high as 20%. The moral is, be careful.
Vasectomy (male sterilisation)	This is an operation which entails the cutting or blocking of the vas deferens (the sperm-carrying tubes). It is a very small incision and takes only five to seven minutes to perform. It can be done on an out-patient basis, under local anaesthetic. The man can continue to have a normal sex life afterwards. It does not interfere with his ability to 'come' or enjoy sex. But after the operation the couple need to use a method of contraception until all the sperm in his testes have been used up (approximately three months). The vasectomy is reversible, with a 50% success rate. However, the pregnancy rate after a vasectomy has been reversed is low. My advice is be 100% sure your family is completed before having it done.

Female methods

**The cap /
diaphragm**

The cap is like a small rubber cup which, when inserted, covers the neck of the womb and prevents the entry of sperm. It initially needs to be fitted by a nurse or doctor who teaches the woman how to insert it herself. Used with spermicide it should be left in place for eight hours after sex, and can be put in up to three hours before intercourse. A popular method for women who do not want to take pills but want to be in control, it can be 95% effective if used properly.

Spermicides

These are chemical substances that come in different forms: cream, jelly, foam and pessary (a tablet inserted into the vagina). They act by killing sperm and forming a protective barrier against the sperm. They cannot be used on their own (the only exception to this could be a menopausal woman over the age of 50). Instead they are a good back-up for the other methods, for example condoms, the cap, IUD, and mini-pill.

IUD (coil)

An IUD is a small object generally made out of plastic (some have copper on) that comes in different shapes and sizes. This IUD is inserted into the woman's womb through the vagina and neck of the womb by a doctor. It can be kept in place for two years, but sometimes can cause cramps or irregular bleeding. It is not fully understood how this method works but it is 97% effective. Spermicide should be used for three months, and then only mid-cycle after that. It is generally not advised for women without any children because of the risk of infection it carries.

The pill

The combined contraceptive pill is made up of two synthetic hormones - oestrogen and progesterone, which prevent the ovaries from releasing an egg. It also makes changes in the lining of the womb and mucus making it difficult to conceive. It is prescribed by a doctor and you start taking it on either the first or the fifth day of your cycle, depending on the brand used. The pill is then taken every day for twenty one days - then stopped for seven days during which the woman has a bleed. It is a reliable method and very convenient. It is 99% effective. It should not be used whilst breastfeeding and certain medications can interfere with its effectiveness, as can diarrhoea or vomiting. Generally you are not safe until you have been taking the pill for seven days and from then you are safe constantly, provided you take it as instructed.

The **mini-pill** (progesterone-only pill): The low dose or mini-pill contains small doses of progesterone. The woman starts taking it on the first day of her period and then at the same time every day after that, taking no breaks. Again it is not clear how it works but it causes changes in the mucus and the fallopian tubes which prevent conception. It has a 5% failure rate approximately. Can cause breakthrough bleeding, and is generally used by women over thirty-five, or who are unsuited to the combined pill. Some doctors advise women to use a spermicide with this method to make it safer.

Vaginal ring

This is new on the market and is called IVR or intra-vaginal ring. It releases low doses of a progesterone hormone called levonorgestrel. This is contained within a ring that is placed in the vagina and 20mgs are released every twenty four hours (compared with the mini-pill's 30-35mgs). The lower dose is effective because the hormone is released locally and doesn't have to go through the woman's system. The ring lasts ninety days and may suit some older women.

Injected contra-ception

Synthetic hormones are injected intramuscularly. The injections may be given every eight to twelve weeks (depending on the brand). It is generally only used where the doctor has found other methods of contraception unsatisfactory. This method is still controversial, but is being used in this country. Problems associated with this method are irregular or heavy bleeding.

Female sterilisation This requires the woman to have an abdominal operation called tubal ligation which involves the cutting or clipping of the fallopian or egg-carrying tubes. Then the egg cannot travel down the tube to meet the sperm. Usually done with a laparoscope (a tiny telescope), it takes about ten minutes and consists of two cuts and needs four sutures. Can be carried out under general or local anaesthesia and usually entails an overnight stay in hospital. Generally, counselling is needed prior to this operation as it is a permanent method. Male sterilisation is a much simpler and cheaper operation.

Resuming sex
after having a baby

The time for having sex after having a baby is when physically and emotionally the woman feels she can cope with it. But having said that, there's no reason why you both can't enjoy loads of kisses and cuddles before full sex starts again. Because let's face it, the last thing on most new mothers' minds is sex. Life revolves around this new baby and the family and sometimes sex just doesn't get a look in, especially if parents are getting a lot of sleepless nights. Parents can no longer make love just when and where they want to spontaneously. And when they go to bed at night they can be just too exhausted for passion. Even for quite some time afterwards many women lack the need or desire for sex. Experts (mostly men) have different theories for this. I think simply that biological necessity in some way turns us towards motherhood and slightly away from loverhood to ensure the species survives and to me that's logical. A lot of adjustments have to be made to fit enjoyable sex and parenthood together.

A parent and a lover?

* Many women feel unattractive and shapeless after having a baby. It's hard to feel sexy if you don't feel good about yourself. So concentrate on giving yourself a **good self-image and spoil yourself.**

* **Exercise daily**, take an interest in how you look. Partners should encourage this by being warm and encouraging and loving (not critical).

* A women may have a mental block about the pain and trauma of childbirth. She can be genuinely frightened of having sex. Do share your feelings with your partner!

* Parenthood can be full of overwhelming emotions. Maybe you feel you just can't fit sex in - talk about it.

* Make sure you still have **time together** to devote to each other. Don't forget to go out on a 'date' regularly together as a couple.

Sex itself

* It is important that the first attempts at intercourse after childbirth should be **controlled by the woman** - otherwise she may be frightened or feel vulnerable in case she feels any pain or discomfort.

* You may prefer to have sex with the woman in the uppermost position, that is, once the man is firm he lies

on his back. The woman can kneel over him (legs either side), then lower herself very gently onto the erect penis (the man can help to guide the penis in if necessary). Then because the woman is in control she need have no fear and can stop any time she desires. Some women may even prefer a side-to-side position - it's up to you.

* At first being this may be enough. Movement may not occur at the first few sessions. Only when the woman is ready should gentle movements be initiated, thrusting only at a later stage when the woman feels more confident.

* It may help to use **lubrication** at first, such as KY jelly or even pure vegetable or fruit oil.

* If too worried to have full sex, go for gentle dilation and masturbation, to yourself or by your partner.

* Do your best to create a warm relaxed **sensual atmosphere** for sex - the role of the partner should be devoted, undemanding and loving and he should state in words 'just tell me to stop if it hurts and I don't mind, I just want to please you'.

* Do use a form of **contraception** - it is extremely common to get pregnant within the first six months of having a baby.

Sex and parenthood

* Adjust sex to suit your needs even if that means doing it quickly sometimes.

* Get a **lock** on the bedroom door and use it.

* Learn to ignore pleadings and yelling from the other side (unless definitely in need, of course).

* **Be flexible.** Make love at different times and in different ways, in different places.

* Occasionally **indulge each other**, book a babysitter, go away for a romantic weekend or night. Or as the song says 'lay the blanket on the ground', or the car in the garage would do.

* Encourage your children to be sociable and outgoing, encourage lots of out of the house activities, clubs and sports that involve outings.

* Don't expect too much! Sex life does change, especially with very young children around. But don't worry, passionate nights have not gone forever.

* If experiencing sexual difficulties there are books that may help, or get in touch with your doctor if you're having physical problems. Or see a sexual counsellor if you'd just like to talk the whole thing out as it can be a combination of many factor. (See the recommended reading at the back of this book for details).

Parents
need sleep too!

If your children are continually disturbing your sleep, nearly all sleeping problems can be remedied by straightforward techniques. There is an end to it, a light at the end of the tunnel - so don't despair (see **Sleeping problems**). During the early years of parenthood do make sleep a priority - get it when you can day and/or night.

Look at your bedroom again. It is an extremely important room. It needs to be warm but well ventilated with comfortable easy colours, not too noisy and with a good bed. A very large bed and good mattress is vitally important and worth investing in (it is also more comfortable if you get little visitors in your bed at night). Have a comfortable nightie or pyjamas (or skin will do). Sleep deprivation can be torture - it is now thought that the real function of sleep is to keep our brains healthy, so no wonder we feel like we're going mad if we don't get enough sleep. Here's a few natural solutions to ensure we parents get our fair share of sleep.

Tips   * Check your **lifestyle, diet**, look closely at your **relationship** and revise your **exercise programme**. What needs changing? Make the changes you think necessary.

* If your general health is not 100%, consider a **medical check-up**, including a urinalysis, blood checks, and for women a smear test.

* Eat **balanced regular meals**, a light evening meal before 6:00pm if possible. Take lots of **fresh air** and **exercise** in the day.

* **Avoid stimulants** - tea, coffee, tobacco after 6:00pm.

* Be careful of **alcohol** - it can make you sleepy but then wake you up a couple of hours later.

* Have a warm relaxing bath followed by an all over massage (lovely). Drop a few drops of **lavender oil** in the bath or on your pillow (Marjoram oil can be used but it is very strong: one to two drops only or it may give you nightmares).

* Do **stretching exercises** for two minutes before getting into bed.

* Ensure your bedroom is **well ventilated**, and **dim the lights**.

* Take a warm glass of **milk**. The calcium contained in the milk is nature's tranquilliser. The tryptophan in milk will help you sleep.

* Try a **herb tea** for your evening drink. Or try a cup of tea brewed from a heaped teaspoon of any of the following herbs: camomile, rosemary, spearmint, passion flower, skull cap.

* Learn a **relaxation technique**. Get comfortable lying down in a warm, quiet place (can be done sitting if necessary). Begin breathing slowly out first, with gentle slow breaths. Direct your thoughts to each part of your body in turn. Starting from the feet and toes, relax each muscle (tense then release or turn out of usual position, then to normal if it helps you achieve a relaxed muscle). Work right up your body slowly. Take time to relax the tense areas such as the neck, shoulders, jaw and forehead. This skill can be learned in many ways through yoga, Transcendental Meditation, books (see the back of this book for details). Start slowly. You don't expect immediate results. Relaxation is an art - go slowly and easily.

* Create your own particular night time pattern and routine. For example bath, hot milk, little read of a book, relaxation technique, sleep.

* Avena Sativa is a non-addictive remedy and aids relaxation and sleeping. It is available from health food stores and chemists.

* Try a sleeping pillow stuffed with dried hops.

* Go through the day backwards in your mind as you fall asleep (like a camera running backwards).

* Tapes with **water sounds**, sounds of the ocean waves or womb sounds can help babies and parents to sleep (see the back of this book for details).

Childcare alternatives

If both parents work outside the home then you need to look at the childcare alternatives available to you well in advance of actually having your baby. Look at your type of employment. Is there any way for parents to stagger their working hours, to minimise the outside help necessary? You need to look again at many aspects of your life, and work out what the ideal situation is for you both, taking into consideration your new addition to the family. Whoever looks after your family, whatever your financial situation, I always feel it is best to pay the top level of the childcare 'going rate'. Our children are the most precious gifts we could ever have and the people who care for them should be paid their worth for this exceptionally important job. So whichever type of child minder you choose to suit your family's needs, show them how much their kindness is appreciated and never 'cut corners' with your childcare. Care for them and they will care for your children but never put up with neglect of their childcare duties, however nice they may seem to you. Make them part of your family but always remember there is also a professional side to the relationship. Once rules are established in the beginning all should go well. A good child minder whom your children love is a great find - treat her/him very well and the relationship will be rewarding on all sides.

Childcare choices

* Look around your own **family**: is there anyone who would be interested in minding your children? If so pay them well, don't abuse them just because they are members of your family. They still need to be paid for time and effort.

* Talk with your **employer**. These days they are more likely to be **flexible** with hours, **job sharing** and **nursery schemes**. Have they any schemes or ideas for working parents?

Childminders

* Unless s/he is a relative, a childminder should be **registered** and should have no more than three children under five to care for. This can give your children company and keep them in a home-type environment (check out safety features as in creche facilities). The pay is usually reasonable and depends on area and facilities.

* Some childminders will care for children in your home, or others with their own children prefer to do it in their own. Pick the one to suit you. Recommendation from friends is often a good way of feeling secure about your choice.

Creches * Are again reasonable in price but numbers are higher; it depends on the age of your child and how much attention s/he requires. Bear in mind the following:

* Check **safety**. Are there guards around heaters? Are stair gates in place? Is it generally tidy and clean?

* **Atmosphere**: do the children seem to be happy and contented? Are any left alone to cry? Do they have plenty of space to play, do they ever get taken to the park? Is there any water play, or is it so tidy the children cannot relax?

* Ask about the day-to-day arrangements, is **food** supplied or not, what are the **hours**, what is the **cost**?

* The **ratio** of childminders to children is very important. There should be at least one adult to eight children.

* Ask what **qualifications** the childminders have. Are they adults or untrained youngsters?

* In the nursery itself look for **fire exits** and the number of **toilets**.

* Ask about **insurance** and **registration**. Do they belong to the national creche/nursery association?

* Have they a **first aid box**?

* Do you like the leader? Is she **approachable** and **friendly**?

* It is always best to stay with the children on the first morning at least, to accustom them to the new surroundings. Stay less the second day and so on, but go earlier if they seem happy enough.

* Creches and childminders tend to be cheaper in country areas.

Au pairs * Your house needs to be large enough to fit another person comfortably.

* S/he needs enough English or Irish to be understood by you and your children.

* S/he should have a **pleasant disposition** - pick one who smiles a lot. S/he should show willingness to be **affectionate** with children and be **eager to help**.

* S/he should give you knowledge of background, family, education, age, experience with children (there are always exceptions, but as a general guideline those who are the 'only' child or the youngest in the family would not be my first choice).

* It is probably best to go through **agencies** initially, although once you establish a good relationship with an au pair s/he may recommend a friend for next time.

* Au pairs get decent pocket money, all board and lodging and two afternoons and evenings free each week plus the weekend. If you want them to work more the pay goes up.

A full time * A good choice if both parents work long hours outside
nanny or the home and, of course, if you can afford one.
housekeeper * S/he can either live in completely or just go home weekends.

* The problem is finding a good one. You can go to an **agency** if you can afford to, which gives you some security. It can be costly but worth it. You could also **advertise** in a newspaper, local rag, shop window or just ask around. The following tips will help you to have a good relationship with your nanny/housekeeper.

* At the **interview**, ask about age, present job, previous jobs or relevant experience, health problems, smoking, education, hobbies, what salary they expect into their hand, and are they willing to pay PRSI. It is essential to ask for **references**.

* When applicants phone have a list of questions (like above) you want to ask them and a sheet of paper ready made out to record answers, then make a short-list to interview. During the interview ask questions like what friends s/he has in your area, if s/he drinks alcohol, what does s/he do in her spare time, has s/he a medical card. Explain all that the job entails, being as truthful as you can. You need to find out if s/he is **capable** and has **common sense**.

* When you have chosen the right person to suit your needs write down the **terms of employment** and state that s/he is only to be made permanent if all goes well after one to three months.

* Do make sure that **a private room** with good facilities is provided. A portable TV would be a good idea.

* **Salaries** vary greatly on top of that s/he has free board and lodgings. A good nanny is worth every penny. Just be sure to get the right one.

* Register yourself as an employer to the Inspector of Taxes. They'll send you lots of booklets, most of which you don't need. Don't be frightened by all the paper work. Just write and organise yearly payments of PRSI.

* At first do write down a **plan** of the daily routine. It helps you and the nanny but hopefully s/he will not need it for very long. It just gives them and you a bit of confidence, too much verbal instruction can be confusing and forgotten or misunderstood.

* Always explain the full workings of your house and have a list of telephone numbers on a board. For example, your work number, a relative's, a neighbour's, a doctor, emergency numbers.

* There are many agencies which will supply more information about childcare. Some supply au pairs or nannies, or a person doing the training course may need a family as s/he is training.

* For names and addresses see the list at the back of this book or advertise yourself.

* Finally always be kind and fair in your dealings with childminders. This kindness usually returns to you or more importantly to your children. It is a very under-rated profession, and one of the most important.

Traditions

Memories are wonderful things. The satisfaction we get from records, pictures, and other things associated with our children's babyhood is amazing. As they get older you can regret not keeping their little booties or preserving a special moment by recording it on video tape. Make the effort to treasure these moments whilst you can. Observe special days, keep birthdays, anniversaries, prepare special menus. Make life special. Give your child a sense of belonging to a wonderful family, a unique family whatever the size. Life and family traditions are what we make them! Let your child know how lucky s/he is to be born into such a wonderful family. Plan occasions together. Have black and white parties, horror parties, space parties, character parties - celebrate!

The birth - start as you mean to go on

* Firstly make a **diary** of your pregnancy, labour and birth.

* Take a **photograph of the baby's nursery** before s/he arrives.

* Take a photograph of your tummy when pregnant and then holding the baby after the birth - it makes a lovely 'before and after' picture.

* Make a little **Time Capsule** of the day of the baby's birth. For example, collect items like: a newspaper from the day of birth; a grocery receipt showing prices; a train ticket, bus ticket or postage stamps; a set of coins with the year of birth.

* Make a little **scrapbook** for baby, collecting items like: baby's identity bracelet; a lock of hair; the press announcement; a baby announcement card; telegrams and cards that arrived; a pressed flower from ones you received after the birth; photographs of baby with the nurse who delivered her/him; baby's weight gain and feeding chart. The list is endless, add in your own special ones.

* It's lovely to keep a print of baby's tiny **hands** and **feet**.

* Put **baby's first gurgles** on tape. Buy a blank tape and record the first sounds, words and sentences. It becomes a record of how the baby's speech developed - great to play when s/he's twenty-one.

* Parents (especially mothers) tend to sing a certain special **lullaby** as their own expression of caring and love - tape it or at least write down the name (my mother sang *Lily Marlene* to me).

* Start a **baby portrait gallery**. Collect pictures of the members of your family as babies.

* Get an **astrological prediction** plan of baby's life (and have a laugh together later when none come true).

* **Invest for baby**, most banks do special accounts for children, give free piggy banks, or even hippopotamus savings banks. Put any gifts of money in and keep the pig as a keepsake. Newborn babies are often given 'lucky money' - keep it as a memento or bank it.

* **Plant a tree** in the garden for each child. Better still every year if you can find the space it will be good for the environment. Choose a hardy long lasting tree, oak, apple, rose.

Later on * Preserve baby's **first shoe** as a silver ornament (fill them with plaster of Paris and spray with silver later).

* Get a large clip frame, glass and hardboard, and take a photograph every month. Arrange them all on the hardboard and keep a **photographic first year** of your baby's life on your wall.

* The **tooth fairy** must visit if a tooth is lost - clever parents put it in a cloth handkerchief with a knot in for easy access later on.

* **Tapes** of all occasions are a great idea. For example, you could record feeding time, or a daily event that could be fun to listen to later. Record all family events, celebrations, or record an ordinary day of talk, songs and activities to send to distant relatives.

* Record the child **telling a story**.

* Photograph everything. Grab the moment. Don't run out of film.

* Keep notes of all your child's great **sayings**. I remember my first daughter's very first sentence.

* One idea I am especially fond of is **writing a letter** to your children each year. Put generally what happened during that year. How much they grew, their accomplishments, what happened in the family, how much you love them. They'll become treasured keepsakes.

* Pick a time when nothing is going on and have a very **Merry Unbirthday party** with presents and fun for all.

* Of course every year **Santa** must be sent a letter either up the chimney or in the post. Don't forget to leave him Christma cake, beer and a carrot for his reindeer.

* Don't forget that a child can have **free wishes** on certain occasions, for example the first strawberry of the season, the first stir of the Christmas pudding, a caught falling autumn leaf or a shooting star. Try to find out what the wish is and help it come true.

* Each parent could take each child out alone to their 'special place' together for lunch once a year.

* Have your very own father's or mother's day different from the commercial one so it is really your family's own day. Make your own cards etc.

* Start a collection of dolls or cars and add one to them each birthday.

* At birthdays get all the guests to write their best wishes on the tablecloth and keep it. Use it every year, keep adding names in all fashions and colours.

* Encourage them to make a *Book About Me* at around the age of five. Help a little, the result can be incredible.

* Do use the **post**. Make it a usual thing to send pictures, drawings, notes etc to relatives home and away.

* Allow the whole family to have a bet on special races, (ours is the Grand National) - 50p to win or each way can make it a great fun event - have a picnic too.

* Once a year (or more often) get a special painting or collage that your child has created framed, so you can appreciate their artistic development.

* Celebrate a pet's birthday. In our house we have birthdays for Sammy the fish, Coco the dog, and Bosco the cat.

* Have a **special family dinner** once a week. Do it nicely with napkins, three courses, table manners, wine for the adults - the lot! It's fun but it also prepares them for the outside world.

* Always encourage the children to **make gifts** for others. They can wrap them in their own drawings, make a card, and even use an old photo as a gift tag.

* Each Christmas let the children pick a toy for a less fortunate child. They could give their pocket money to a charity of their choice.

* Have a **garden fete** or party. Charge guests a small amount, then send the money collected to the local children's hospital.

* On the first day of May, clean your face with early morning dew. It makes you beautiful all year!

* Take a photograph of your child playing, wearing or using the present someone brought for her/him. Send the kind person a 'thank you' note with the picture. Encourage children to send thank you notes written by themselves, for all presents given.

* Have a **family meeting** every week, to laugh, talk, tell news, air grievances.

* Have a **treasure hunt** for birthday presents. If near a beach, Captain McGinty may leave a bottle with a treasure map inside - we have great fun doing this.

* Have an **egg party** at Easter. All the children can decorate the eggs together, and take them home afterwards. Or try out Bob's Bunny Trail: egg treasures are found all over the house and garden, the last one found is the biggest. Leave clues in rhyme as to the whereabouts of each egg. (For the plotting parents it is best to put the egg in place and go backwards, working out the clues.)

* **Hire a video** to record special events - it is a worthwhile investment and a positive pleasure to look back over the years.

Recommended reading

Balaskas, Janet *Active Birth* Unwin Paperbacks.

Brown and Faulder *Treat Yourself To Sex* Penguin.

Carson, Dr Paul *How To Cope With Your Child's Allergies* Sheldon Press.

Carson, Dr Paul *How To Cope With Your Child's Asthma* Sheldon Press.

Carson, Dr Paul *How To Cope With Your Child's Hyperactivity* Sheldon Press.

Comfort, A *The Joy Of Sex* Quartet.

Elliot, M *Willow Street Kids* Piccolo. A story of a group of friends and how they ensure their security/safety, for children aged over 8.

Elliott, M *Keeping Safe* NEC. A common sense guide for parents on talking with children about problems such as bullying, drugs and sexual abuse.

ERIC (Enuresis Resource and Information Center) *Eric's Wet to Dry Bedtime Book*. For children - available through ERIC - see addresses.

Ferber, Dr R *Solve Your Child's Sleep Problems* DK.

Foresight *Guidelines For Future Parents*. Useful guide published by the association of pre-conceptual care - see addresses.

Herron, A and D McGinley *The Family Handbook Of Sex Education* Irish Mentor Books. For parents.

Jennings, G *Successful Day Nursery Management* Attic Press.

Lennet, R and B Crane *It's OK To Say No* Thorsons. Bedtime stories on personal safety for children.

Liddy, R and D Walsh *Surviving Sexual Abuse* Attic Press.

MacFarlene and McPherson *The Diary Of A Teenage Health Freak* Oxford Paperbacks. Age Teens. General life and health guide, very amusing. Also a second book called *I'm A Health Freak Too*, very popular with teenagers.

Madders, J *Stress and Relaxation* Positive Health.

Maher, Chi *Sex Education and Health Matters for Girls* Attic Press.

Meredith, S and R Gee *Understanding the Facts of Life* Osbourne. Age 10+. In two sections - can be bought separately.

Our New Baby Macdonald. Children's book explaining new arrival.

Parker, Steve *The Body and How It Works* Dorling Kindersley. Age 8+.

Pickering, Lucienne *Boy Talk* Cassell. Age 10-12.

Pickering, Lucienne *Girl Talk* Cassell. Age 10-12.

Pickering, Lucienne *Parents Listen* Cassell. Guide for parents.

RFGF Resources *Red Flag Green Flag People* A saftey programme using colouring books for children.

Sheffield, M *Where Do Babies Come From* Jonathon Cape. Age 5-10.

Stone, Rosemary *Loving Encounters - A Young Person's Guide to Sex* Lions. Age teens.

Stones, Rosemary *Where Babies Come From* Dinosaur. Age 4-8.

Welford, H *Toilet Training and Bedwetting* Thorsons.

Young, Carol *Crying For Help: How to Cure Your Baby of Colic* Thorsons.

Useful addresses

ACTION AGAINST ALLERGY 23-24 George's Street, Richmond, Surrey TW9 1JY.

AFASIC 347 Central Markets, Smithfield, London EC1A 9NH. Tel (071) 2363632/2366487. Provides information for parents of speech-impaired children.

ASSOCIATION FOR IMPROVEMENT OF MATERNITY SERVICES (AIMS) 1 Tivoli Parade, Tivoli Road, Dun Laoghaire Co Dublin. 21 Iver Lane, Bucks, SLO 9LH England.

ASSOCIATION FOR THE WELFARE OF CHILDREN IN HOSPITAL (Ireland) Brookwood, Tubber, Lucan, Co. Dublin. Tel (01) 889278/281157.

ASSOCIATION OF POST-NATAL ILLNESS 7 Gowen Ave, London SW6 6HR.

ASTHMA SOCTIEY OF IRELAND 24 Anglesea Street, Dublin 2. Tel (01) 716551.

COLLEGE OF SPEECH THERAPISTS 6 Lechmore Road, London NW2. Produces a leaflet on teaching your child to talk.

COMPLEMENTARY MEDICINE ADVICE NUMBER (01) 388196 (Ireland).

CRY-SIS London WC1N 3XX. Tel (071) 4045011.

DEPARTMENT OF HEALTH AND SOCIAL SERVICES (DHSS) offices throughout the UK, consult local telephone directory.

DEPARTMENT OF SOCIAL WELFARE PO Box 1650, Store Street, Dublin 1. Tel (01) 786466. (See telephone directory for regional offices).

DUBLIN WELL WOMAN CENTRE 73 Lower Leeson Street, Dublin 2. Tel (01) 610083 or 610086.

EARTHWATCH 1 Harbour View, Bantry, West Cork. Tel (027) 50968.

ENURESIS RESOURCE AND INFORMATION CENTER (ERIC) 65 St Michael's Hill, Bristol BS2 8DZ. Tel (0202) 556920. For information on bed wetting.

FAMILY PLANNING ASSOCIATION 27-35 Mortimer Street, London W1N 7RJ. Tel (071) 6367866. Contraceptive advice branches throughout country.

FANNINS 14/16 Redmond's Hill, Dublin 2. Tel (01) 782211. Suppliers of bed wetting alarms.

FEDERATION OF UNMARRIED PARENTS AND THEIR CHILDREN 36 Upper Rathmines Road, Dublin 6. Tel (01) 964155.

FORESIGHT The Assocation of Pre-conceptual Care, The Old Vicarage, Church Lane, Whitley, Godalming, Surrey GU8 5PN. Tel (0428) 684500.

FRIENDS OF THE EARTH 26-28 Underwood Street, London NI 7JQ. Tel (071) 4901555.

GINGERBREAD GROUP 35 Wellington Street, London WC2E 7BN. Tel (01) 2400953.

GINGERBREAD IRELAND Top Floor, 12 Wicklow Street, Dublin 2. Tel (01) 710291 10:00am-5:00pm.

HOME BIRTH INFORMATION CENTER OF IRELAND The Mews, 4 Leinster Road, Dublin 6. Tel (01) 977342.

HYPERACTIVE CHILDREN'S SUPPORT GROUP 71 Whyke Lane, Chichester, Sussex. Tel (0903) 725182. 4 Elton Park, Sandycove, Co Dublin. Tel (01) 808766.

IRISH ALLERGY TREATMENT AND RESEARCH ASSOCIATION PO Box 1067, Churchtown, Dublin 14.

IRISH CHILDBIRTH TRUST c/o Mary Linnane, Vigo Lodge, Killaboy, Ennis, Co. Clare.

IRISH FAMILY PLANNING ASSOCIATION (IFPA) 36-37 Lower Ormond Quay, Dublin 1. Tel (01) 730877.

IRISH PARENTS ASSOCIATION FOR GIFTED CHILDREN Carmichael House, North Brunswick Street, Dublin 7. Tel (01) 390590/308953.

IRISH SOCIETY OF SPEECH THERAPISTS PO Box 1344, Dublin 4. Tel (01) 803142.

LA LECHE LEAGUE PO Box 1280, Raheny, Dublin 5. Tel (01) 463248 or (051) 55784. PO Box BM3424, London WC1N 3XX. Tel (071) 4055011 or (071) 2421278. Breastfeeding help and information, 24-hour counselling service. For local groups see your telephone directory.

LULLABABY Parish Lane, Kings Thorn, Hereford HR2 8AH. Tel (0981) 540288. Lullababy supply tapes for pregnancy and baby womb sounds.

MILK ALLERGY SELF-HELP GROUP (MASH) 4 Queen Anne's Grove, Bush Hill Park, Enfield, Middlesex EN1 2JP. Tel (081) 3602348.

MINISTRY OF AGRICULTURE, FISHERIES AND FOOD 3/10 Whitehall Place, London SW1A 2HH. (071) 2703000. For the most recent *Look at the Label* booklet.

MISCARRIAGE ASSOCIATION PO Box 24, Ossett, West Yorkshire WF5 9XG. Tel (0924) 264579.

MISCARRIAGE SUPPORT GROUP IRELAND c/o Ms Hilary Frazer, 27 Kennilworth Road, Dublin 6. Tel (01) 972938.

MYSTERIES NEW AGE CENTRE 9-11 Monmouth Street, Covent Garden, London WC2 HDA. Relaxation and womb sounds tapes.

NATIONAL ASSOCIATION OF PARENTS WITH SLEEPLESS CHILDREN PO Box 33, Prestwood Gt Missenden, Bucks NH16 OSZ.

NATIONAL ASSOCIATION OF THE OVUALTION METHOD OF IRELAND 36 Washington Street, Cork. Tel (021) 272213. 16 North Great George's Street, Dublin 2. Tel (01) 786156. Centres throughout the country.

NATIONAL CHILDBIRTH TRUST Alexandra House, Oldham Terrace, Acton, London W3 6NH. Tel (081) 9928637.

NATIONAL COUNCIL FOR ONE PARENT FAMILIES 255 Kentish Town Road, London NW5 2LX. Tel (071) 2671361.

NATIONAL ECZEMA SOCIETY c/o 43 Galtymore Road, Drimnagh, Dublin 12. Tel (01) 557807. Tavistock House, East Tavistock Square, London WC1H 9SR. Tel (071) 3884097.

NATIONAL SOCIAL SERVICES BOARD 71 Lower Leeson Street, Dublin 2. Tel (01) 616422. Provides a list of COMMUNITY INFORMATION CENTRES throughout Ireland.

NATURESWAY in Dublin, Cork and Kilkenny for natural remedies. Tel (056) 65402 for details of postal service.

PARENTS ALONE RESOURCE CENTRE 325 Bunratty Road, Coolock, Dublin 5. Tel (01) 481872.

PARENTS UNDER STRESS Carmichael House, North Brunswick Street, Dublin 7. Tel (01) 733500.

POST-NATAL DISTRESS GROUP c/o Ann O'Connor, 2 Dara Crescent, Celbridge, Co Kildare.

PRE-SCHOOL PLAYGROUP ASSOCIATION 19 Wicklow Street, Dublin 2. Tel (01) 719245. 61-63 King's Cross Road, London WC1 X9LL. Tel (071) 8330991.

ST JOHN'S AMULANCE BRIGADE OF IRELAND 29 Upper Leeson Street, Dublin 4. Tel (01) 688077. Organises classes in First Aid.

STILLBIRTH AND NEONATAL DEATH SOCIETY PO Box 6, Dun Laoghaire, Co Dublin. Tel (01) 831910/859791. 28 Portland Place, London W1N 4DE. Tel (071) 4365881.

THE FOOD AND CHEMICAL ALLERGY ASSOCIATION 27 Ferringham Lane, Ferring-by-the-Sea, West Sussex BN12 5NB. Tel (0903) 41178.

THE NATIONAL ASSOCIATION FOR THE WELFARE OF CHILDREN IN HOSPITAL Argle House, 29-31 Euston Road, London NW1 2SD. Tel (071) 8332041.

TWINS AND MULTIPLE BIRTH ASSOCIATION c/o 59 Sunnyside, Worksop, Nottinghamshire S81 7LN. Tel (0909) 479250.

VOCAL 336 Brixton Road, London SW9 7AA. Tel (071) 2744029. Information on all organisations concerned with communication problems.

WORKING MOTHER ASSOCIATION 77 Holloway Road, London N7 8JZ. Tel (071) 7005771.

Index